THE PRICE OF FAITH

THE PRICE OF FAITH

Exploring Our Choices
about Money and Wealth

Marie T. Cross

Geneva Press
Louisville, Kentucky

© 2002 Marie T. Cross

Scripture quotations from the New Revised Standard Version of the Bible are copyright © 1989 by the Division of Christian Education of the National Council of the Churches of Christ in the U.S.A. and are used by permission.

Book design by Sharon Adams
Cover design by Night & Day Design

First edition
Published by Geneva Press
Louisville, Kentucky

This book is printed on acid-free paper that meets the American National Standards Institute Z39.48 standard. ∞

PRINTED IN THE UNITED STATES OF AMERICA

03 04 05 06 07 08 09 10 11 — 10 9 8 7 6 5 4 3 2

Library of Congress Cataloging-in-Publication Data
Cross, Marie T., 1945–
    The price of faith : exploring our choices about money
and wealth / Marie T. Cross—1st ed.
        p. cm.
    Includes bibliographical references.
    ISBN 0-664-50216-4
        1. Christian giving—Presbyterian Church (U.S.A.)
2. Presbyterian Church (U.S.A.)—Finance. I. Title.

BX9189.5.C76 2002
248'.6—dc21   2001040570

Contents

Preface

Almost every aspect of life in American culture is affected in some way by money. This book is an introduction to the study of faith and money. The topics I have chosen may spark your interest and lead to questions I have not asked. Your experience—your walk of faith, your work, family circumstances, goals and desires, your congregation's mission, membership, and setting—may lead to more study in one area than another. More importantly, this book will help you learn different ways of putting beliefs about faith and money into practice.

In the process of my study of the issues of faith and money, I encountered other related subjects I still want to explore. One in particular is the offering plate, its theology and its history. What is the significance of when, how, and by whom the offering is collected? There is a history of offering receptacles to explore—plates, boxes, basins, and bags. There is also a history of theology concerning the place of the offering in the worship service. More than that, there is the symbolism of the offering plate and what it expresses of our faith, our gratitude, and our relationship with God.

Another interesting study would be to focus on church leaders and to conduct a statistical study of congregational life, leadership models, and actual habits of giving. How would the spiritual life and general "health" of particular congregations compare with levels of giving in the church? What would be the correlation between the practices of financial stewardship of church members and what the leadership teaches and/or preaches about financial steward-ship? What are the giving practices of those same leaders, and what do they support with their own resources?

Still other subjects to study are issues of investments, vocational choice, and teaching children and youth about money. The list could certainly go on.

This book attempts to bring the discussion of stewardship into the life and work of the church, perhaps to challenge the choices we make about money and wealth, and in the process to help us grow together in faith.

An additional note is that there are occasional references to resources and statements of faith from the Presbyterian Church (U.S.A.). They are given as examples or sources to be helpful at particular points, but do not affect the use of this book or the session plans in it. The book is fitting or adapt-able for all Christians whose goal is to live faithfully. Simi-lar statements and resources from other denominations can be found through governing body offices, resource centers, and Web sites.

My thanks to many people who have offered their support, expertise, and helpful comments throughout the process of writing this book—my husband, Steve, my family, and friends; also my former colleagues in the Stewardship Edu-cation Program Area of the Presbyterian Church (U.S.A.) and Professors Amy Plantinga Pauw and David C. Hester of Louisville Presbyterian Theological Seminary.

PART ONE   Faith and Money

Chapter 1

Why Talk about Faith and Money?
An Introduction

A number of years ago I had the opportunity to hear Robert Wood Lynn speak at a conference for pastors and denominational staff who work in stewardship and mission funding. Formerly with the Lilly Endowment, Inc., Lynn is a retired foundation executive and independent scholar in Portland, Maine, and much of his work has had to do with money, the church, and faith. He has noted that, in general, there is a reluctance to talk about these things in the church and among religious writers and scholars.

> I am frequently disappointed by theologians who write books on stewardship, because if you read those books and look for any clear, sustained discussion about money, you will not find it except in an incidental fashion. . . . In fact, the authors of these books have almost converted the theme of stewardship into a synonym for Christian responsibility without once really exploring what it means to give money or think about money.[1]

Robert Wuthnow, in his book *God and Mammon in America*, discovered the same attitude from his research.

> Observers who have lived in other societies note that Americans are much more reluctant to talk about

3

money than people elsewhere. . . . Religion is probably
one of the sources of this taboo. . . . If religious leaders
want to help people apply their faith to their financing,
therefore, it seems clear . . . that breaking through the bar-
rier against talking about money must be a first step.[2]

While stewardship itself is a word often heard in the church,
money is seldom discussed in terms of moral and ethical
decisions and daily lifestyle choices.

This concern about money and the church comes not so
much from the reality that funds are shrinking in mainline
Protestant denominations, but from concerns about the role
and the future of the church in a consumer society. Although
a holistic understanding of stewardship is important, it is time
to deal with money and what it means for us in all aspects of
our lives, including our participation in the life of the church
and our own expressions of personal faith.

A study of faith and money requires looking at all that
money touches upon and means for us. Money is more than
just the cash, checks, or credit cards we have in hand. It signifies, at least to some extent, our sense of value and importance, our identity, and our security. So the subject of
this book extends beyond money itself. It includes the meaning of wealth and an understanding of what is "enough." It
includes lifestyles and the "stuff" we buy and accumulate.
And it includes all the choices implicit in earning, spending,
saving, and giving money. It is about *faith* and money, and
the church must be a place where we can talk about these difficult, complex issues and decisions.

Educational Opportunities in the Church

Most often the opportunities for adult education are in small
group studies that take place on Sunday mornings, weekday
evenings, and retreats, and they allow for people to discuss
the subject of faith and money. Church committee meeting

times may sometimes lend themselves to education. In spite of the usual pressure to hear reports and make decisions, such meetings can begin with a brief study using one of the session plans. The study could be planned in such a way that it would serve as the opening devotional time for a series of meetings. Participating in mission projects and talking around the tables at fellowship dinners may also be occasions for education if the time is scheduled and the discussions are guided. Perhaps such table conversations could serve to promote and introduce a class or retreat scheduled for another time when there would be a more extended, in-depth study.

Take a look at your congregation's calendar and think creatively about when and how often the subject of stewardship can be discussed and study can occur. Consider the whole year, not just when it is time for the annual financial pledge campaign. Along with adult studies, plan for youth and children's education as well.

Preachers may also find the chapters on the biblical and theological foundations helpful for sermons. Some of the case studies or other parts of the session plans offer illustrative stories and quotations. Year-round stewardship preaching not only serves as a reminder but also builds a foundation for a pledge campaign.

Year-round financial stewardship is, in fact, an important goal for the church and for each one of us.

More about This Book and the Session Plans

Chapter 2 is about the contemporary context of church and culture that gives both the impetus and the rationale for studying faith and money. It offers a discussion about the definition of stewardship and the use of this term in the life of the church, as well as commentary on the willingness or reluctance of church leaders to talk about issues of financial stewardship. It also deals briefly with recent research among mainline Protestant churches in America regarding religious giving. There is some urgency for us, as individuals and as the church, at this time in history. As the church and as part of a developing global economy, we need to be a voice of conscience and vision, raising questions and searching for ways to live with justice, integrity, and faith.

Part Two (chapters 3 through 8) offers the biblical and theological foundations for a study of faith and money. The number of Scripture texts that deal either explicitly or implicitly with stewardship is almost unending, especially when stewardship is defined fully as a descriptive term for discipleship. Even when stewardship is narrowed to the meaning of money, wealth, and possessions, the possibilities are numerous.

Chapter 3 begins with an introduction to the search for texts that specifically refer to stewardship and then proposes reading the Bible from a stewardship perspective.

Chapters 4 through 8 are based on five themes that provide a framework for the session plans, which are found in Part Three. These themes are Creator and Creation, Trust and Hope, Managing Money, Giving and Asking, and The Household of God. Each of the five chapters includes related biblical texts and references to creeds, confessions, and commentaries from various sources. Additional concepts and images of stewardship are explored in order to understand the attitudes, beliefs, and practices surrounding the use of money and to look at implications for a holistic understanding of stewardship.

Each theme has something to say about our relationship with God, the choices we make in daily living, the lifestyle we have adopted, and our response to God's call upon our lives. These themes raise questions about ownership, power, vocation, economic justice, generosity, and gratitude. Chapter 8, "The Household of God," highlights what it means to teach, learn, and live out what we believe about stewardship together as the church.

With each of the five biblical/theological themes covered in chapters 4–8, a correlation is made with one or more of the ten session plans. A box with the title and purpose statement of each plan has been inserted where relevant. While each session plan touches on more than one of these biblical/ theological themes, particular connections can be made between certain studies and one of the five themes.

Part Three, "Session Plans for Stewardship Study," begins by explaining how a true education about stewardship is a transformative experience in which our lives are affected by what we learn. Ten session plans are included, along with an introduction describing how the studies may be used in various settings. Each of the session plans can be completed in approximately one hour, though, in most cases, suggestions are given to expand them for a more in-depth study or shorten them to fit the opening of a church meeting.

At the conclusion, a final word is offered on the subject of faith and money—a summary statement and encouragement for all of us to continue the pursuit of learning what it means to be a faithful steward.

NOTES

1. Robert Wood Lynn, *The Reluctant Steward: A Report and Commentary on the Stewardship and Development Study* (Indianapolis: Christian Theological Seminary; St. Meinrad, Ind.: St. Meinrad Seminary, 1992), 30.

2. Robert Wuthnow, *God and Mammon in America* (New York: Free Press, 1994), 138–41.

Chapter 2

Faith and Money—A Challenge for the Church

*The earth is the LORD's and all that is in it,
the world, and those who live in it.*
— Psalm 24:1

Your money or your life?
*Not a simple question, since most people can't
seem to differentiate the two.*
— "Americans and Their Money," Worth

*In this society we not only ask the question
what's its worth or what the person is worth,
but we often judge ourselves by the values
embedded in money.*
— Robert Wood Lynn

*When we see some of our ordinary activities as
Christian practices, we come to perceive how
our daily lives are all tangled up with the
things God is doing in the world.*
— Dorothy C. Bass

Faith and money are two words that are seldom spoken or heard together. Money and all that it can buy, possessions and what they can mean for our social status and personal comfort, wealth and its power to create or control, may all seem irrelevant or disconnected from the piety and practice of Christian faith.

We may be reluctant to talk about financial matters in serious conversations that involve questions and matters of faith, but we as a culture are consumed with concerns about money, and our lives tend to revolve around getting, spending, and having enough of it. Whether or not we think of our ordinary, daily decisions about money as being evidence of our deepest faith convictions, *they are*. Intentional or not, what we are doing reflects what we believe. And what we are doing is not only telling others, but also teaching others.

As the quotations from Scripture and the other references above suggest, faith and money are both part of ordinary living. And if that is so, then faith and money must share integrity with the ways in which we choose to live. Faith and money belong together—in the same sentence.

The challenge for the church, as individuals and as a community, is to bring the conversations—the struggle, confession, embarrassment, guilt, ambiguity, and good intentions—into its life of worship, study, and service.

Defining Stewardship

Money is one aspect of the meaning and practice of stewardship, and stewardship is part of the church's vocabulary. Although the word is used in other areas such as business, politics, and concern for the environment, *stewardship,* for the church, is a biblical and theological term that describes faithful discipleship.

Most often when it is used in church, stewardship refers to finances, budgets, and annual pledge campaigns. The word actually encompasses a holistic understanding of creation as a gift from God. As part of God's created order, we are to be *stewards* of the world within, among, and around us—our bodies, minds, and spirits; our community, the church, and the people of the world; the air, soil, and water, and the creatures who dwell therein; our time, energy, imagination, and talents—and our money, wealth, and possessions.

Douglas John Hall, in what has become a stewardship classic, wrote of stewardship as a metaphor that encompasses the very nature of being a Christian.

> Stewardship must be understood first as descriptive of the being—the very life—of God's people. Deeds of stewardship arise out of the being of the steward.[1]

Stewardship Talk in the Church

The broader understanding of stewardship is not so difficult to preach or teach about as is the particular issue of money. For example, a group of approximately one hundred Presbyterian pastors was surveyed. Altogether, they represented the spectrum of Presbyterian pastors throughout the denomination in terms of age, year of ordination, and size of congregation being served. Ninety-nine percent said they were comfortable or somewhat comfortable preaching sermons about nonmonetary aspects of stewardship. Virtually 100 percent agreed that teaching people to be responsible stewards is an appropriate role for the pastor. Yet only 64 percent were perfectly comfortable preaching about the monetary aspects of stewardship.[2]

On the one hand, the concept of stewardship needs to be expanded for many churchgoers to mean more than the annual budget and regular offerings. On the other hand, we need to overcome our reluctance to talk about money in terms of faith and not just in terms of numbers, projections, and deficits of the congregation's fiscal health. In fact, the financial health of the church or of a person of faith may also say something about spiritual well-being. Giving careful, disciplined attention to beliefs and practices of faith and money necessarily becomes part of the life of faith when stewardship is understood in a holistic sense.

Money and all the issues that emerge from how we earn it, accumulate it, and make decisions about using it or sharing it, must become as much a part of what we talk about in the church as the practices of worship and study. We cannot exclude one part of living from critical examination, and we cannot offer simplistic answers to what it means to be faithful in terms of our money. William Muehl in his book *Why Preach? Why Listen?* gives this example:

> At a conference on stewardship a few years ago, one of the prominent business [persons] present sat through several hours of discussion in stony silence. Then ... finally burst out, "Why do I always get the feeling from preachers that the only Christian thing to do with my business is to sell it and divide the proceeds among the poor?"
>
> I have become persuaded that there are a great many people like my banker friend in our churches today, men and women whose apparent addiction to economic and social advancement reflects not crass materialism but an often unguided, uninformed urge to express creative energies at work within them, energies which traditional preaching does little or nothing to help them understand and harness responsibly. . . . And all that many of us do in our sermons is cluck our tongues critically at so much frantic getting and spending.[3]

We Need to Talk

According to independent studies conducted by Dean Hoge of the Catholic University of America, Sylvia and John Ronsvalle of empty tomb, inc., and Robert Wuthnow of the Center for the Study of American Religion at Princeton University, these are critical times for mainline Protestant churches in America.[4] Declining memberships, loss of cultural status and authority, and decreases in giving pose challenges to the survival and growth of these denominations. Added to the current state of mainline churches is the fact that many Americans are experiencing greater prosperity than ever before, while at the same time there is a growing economic gulf between the rich and the poor. These are issues of personal ethics and corporate responsibility concerning money. Our postindustrial society has come to depend on the consumer. Spending, investing, speculating, and simply shopping involve the transfer of money and raise issues of justice and morality. Money is everywhere in our society, affecting lifestyle, political agendas, workplace relationships, medical care, and everyday hopes and dreams.

> Our moment in history, then, is a time of growing uncertainty, of great personal challenges, and of urgent need. Despite the material prosperity our nation has enjoyed, we are now at a turning point when we need to think more deeply about our priorities. We are concerned about the materialism that surrounds us and the acquisitive values that are being communicated to our children. . . . Our problems as a nation are spiritual as well as material. We must take stock of what our spiritual heritage is telling us and of how we are to be instructed by its counsel.[5]

Now is a significant time for the church. Financial stewardship must be given attention, not so much for the survival of the church's institutions, its structures and hierarchies (which, in fact, are being threatened), but for a vital, viable interpretation of what it means to live faithfully in this time and place.

We are to be *stewards*—caretakers and managers—carefully tending the gifts God has entrusted to us, using them for the benefit of everyone, wisely keeping them to pass on to future generations and creating with God an economy where there is enough for all to survive and enough for all to enjoy. These ways of tending, keeping, and creating are the practices of our faith.

Woven together, Christian practices form a way of life. . . . [This way of life] becomes visible as ordinary people search together for specific ways of taking part in the practice of God, as they faithfully perceive it in the complicated places where they really live.[6]

As we develop habits of faith, they begin to define us in new ways and open up new possibilities for becoming the people and the world God created us to be.

NOTES

At the head of this chapter, the quotation of "Americans and Their Money" is from *Worth,* June 1994 (author: Robert Sullivan). The Robert Wood Lynn quotation is from an interview in *Inside Information,* published by the Alban Institute, 1998. The quotation from Dorothy C. Bass is from *Practicing Our Faith: A Way of Life for a Searching People,* ed. Dorothy C. Bass (San Francisco: Jossey-Bass Publishers, 1997), 8.

1. Douglas John Hall, *The Steward: A Biblical Symbol Come of Age,* rev. ed. (New York: Friendship Press, 1990), 242.

2. *Survey Findings*, from "Spirit of Stewardship: A National Conference for Pastors," October 24–27, 1994. Sponsored by the PC(USA) Foundation, Mission Funding, and Stewardship Program Areas of the Presbyterian Church (U.S.A.) (Louisville, Ky.: Research Services, Presbyterian Church (U.S.A.), 1994).

3. William Muehl, *Why Preach? Why Listen?* (Philadelphia: Fortress Press, 1986), 41–42.

4. Wuthnow, *God and Mammon in America.* John and Sylvia Ronsvalle, *Behind the Stained Glass Windows: Money Dynamics in the Church* (Grand Rapids: Baker Books, 1996). Dean R. Hoge, Charles E. Zech, Patrick H. McNamara, and Michael J. Donahue, *Money Matters: Personal Giving in American Churches* (Louisville, Ky.: Westminster John Knox Press, 1996).

5. Wuthnow, *God and Mammon in America,* 36.

6. Bass and Craig Dykstra, ed., *Practicing Our Faith,* 203.

PART TWO Foundations for Study

Chapter 3

Beginning with the Bible

*T*he Bible is the place to begin a study for developing habits and practices of faith and possibilities for transformation. The story of faith begins with God's creative power and continues through the biblical account of people in relationship with God and one another. Later creeds and confessions of the church and writings and commentaries of faithful individuals have added to the story and to understanding the story. The Bible remains the source, and so a study of faith and money must begin there, too.

The word *steward* or *stewardship* appears 17 (NRSV) to 21 (KJV) to 27 (RSV) times in the Old and New Testaments, depending on how translators chose to deal with Hebrew and Greek terms such as *mesheq*, *'al*, *oikonomia*, and *oikonomos*. Most often the original meaning is that of a manager or someone in charge of a household.

It is interesting that in the Old Testament, the language connotes a relationship, while in the New Testament, steward is a role. The word *'al* is a preposition meaning above, over, or in charge of, and it is used four out of five times in Genesis and in 1 Kings where the translation is "steward." The use of a preposition creates a picture of a relationship between the person who is in charge and whatever is being cared for or managed, *and* a relationship with whoever has placed that person in charge. In the Gospels of Matthew and Luke and in several other places in the New Testament, the words *oikonomia* and *oikonomos* convey the concept or role of a caretaker or manager.

The Old Testament idea of a relationship is helpful, especially when thinking of stewardship as a way of being. In *The Steward: A Biblical Symbol Come of Age*, Douglas John Hall proposed that *being* a steward is a way of being Christian.

> What if stewardship became our very mode of operation, our characteristic stance, our way of being in the world, our means of expressing and confessing our faith—not an addendum, not a means to something else, not an evangelistic come-on, but the very heart of the matter! Is it sheer idealism to think that the church of the Crucified One, crucified for the love of the world, is incapable of such depths of caring?[1]

In his second book about stewardship, Hall developed the idea of relationship as a way of describing that *being*, or living, with one another and nature. It is the relationships we have that make us distinctive among the rest of creation; that is, we are made in the image of God. Human responsibility for dominion (Gen. 1:28) is to be understood within relationships, and these relationships are to reflect the relationship we have with God. So Hall speaks of "being-with-God," "being-with-humankind," and "being-with-nature."

> We mirror the sovereignty of the divine love in our stewardship of the earth. This lifts Christian stewardship well beyond the confines of a pragmatic ethic. . . . We have our commission as a sacred trust that inheres in our new identity—or, more accurately, this old identity into which we are newly born through grace and repentance. We are preservers because the creation is intrinsically good.[2]

The role of the responsible steward is implied in the Old Testament texts, but the idea of a role, rather than a relationship, is more often the way the New Testament deals with stewardship. Some of these Scriptures are the parables of the Laborers in the Vineyard (Matt. 20:1–16) and the Dishonest Steward (Luke 16:1–13); or references in Ephesians (the stewardship of God's grace (KJV 3:2) and 1 Corinthians (stewards of God's mysteries, 4:2). The New Testament word *oikonomos* is the root of such words as economics, ecology, and ecumenical, and these lead to further ideas of faith and money in broader contexts.

The actual number of times the word *steward* or *stewardship* occurs in the Bible is relatively few, so reading the Bible from a perspective of stewardship may be more helpful than simply looking for the words. In addition, we begin to see issues of ownership, possession, wealth, and power emerge from the Psalms, the prophets, New Testament letters, wisdom literature, and other books where we might not think to look at first.

Bible-Based Stewardship

READING THE BIBLE FROM A STEWARDSHIP PERSPECTIVE

Session Plan 1

PURPOSE   The subject of stewardship is found throughout the Bible in texts that deal with money, ownership, and possessions as well as texts where the subject is implicit or understood in a broader sense. This session begins with building a definition of stewardship that includes all aspects of life for which we are called to be stewards and caretakers. It is meant to be an exercise that leads to reading the whole Bible with an expectation of finding lessons about stewardship.

Reading and studying the Bible from a stewardship perspective is our goal. Once we become sensitive to the issues and questions of stewardship and how they impact our lives in both ordinary and significant ways, we cannot help but see and hear things differently from before. The Bible raises our awareness and calls us to roles of responsible stewardship and relationships with God, nature, and all of humanity.

NOTES

1. Hall, *The Steward*, 255–6.
2. Douglas John Hall, *Imagining God: Dominion as Stewardship* (New York: Friendship Press, 1986), 200.

Chapter 4

Creator and Creation

In the beginning when God created the heavens and the earth, the earth was a formless void and darkness covered the face of the deep, while a wind from God swept over the face of the waters. Then God said, "Let there be light," and there was light. And God saw that the light was good.
                                                                    —Genesis 1:1–4a

O LORD, *how manifold are your works!*
In wisdom you have made them all;
the earth is full of your creatures.
                                                                    —Psalm 104:24

*J*ust as the Bible is the place to begin the study of faith and money, Genesis is the place to begin in the Bible: "In the beginning when God created the heavens and the earth" is a statement of faith that all of life belongs to God. All of life's mysteries, magnitude, variety, and possibilities come as gifts from God. Therefore, the source of power and purpose in the world is God, not ourselves. Daily routines and responsibilities, and sometimes the urgent necessities for survival, may lead us to think that we have everything to do with whether or not life goes on. However, the reality is that God is sovereign over all of life. This is Calvin's statement:

21

> We are not our own: let not our reason nor our will there-
> fore sway our plans and deeds. We are not our own: let us
> therefore not set it as our goal to seek what is expedient for
> us according to the flesh. We are not our own: in so far as
> we can, let us therefore forget ourselves and all that is ours.
>
>   Conversely, we are God's: let us therefore live for
> [God] and die for [God]. We are God's: let [God's] wis-
> dom and will therefore rule all our actions. We are God's:
> let all the parts of our life accordingly strive toward [God]
> as our only lawful goal [Rom. 14:8; cf. 1 Cor. 6:19].[1]

Affirmations of God's sovereignty are also found in the Heidelberg Catechism.

> [T]he eternal Father of our Lord Jesus Christ, who out of
> nothing created heaven and earth with all that is in
> them, . . . also upholds and governs them by [God's] eter-
> nal counsel and providence. . . . I trust in [God] so com-
> pletely that I have no doubt that [God] will provide me
> with all things necessary for body and soul.[2]

We *own* nothing; we belong to God. Likewise, our money,
wealth and possessions, and all the "stuff" we have, are not
really *ours*, but are ours to use, care for, and share. When we
can comprehend this, we are relieved of any anxiety we
might have about keeping and saving things for just ourselves. We begin to understand our responsibility for using
wisely what God has given us and finding ways to live alongside others, making the most of what we and they have to
offer.

   Along with the Priestly writer of Genesis, we affirm that
God is the source of life and that life was meant to be good.
This "goodness" is translated into a world where there is
recognition and celebration by everyone of the whole variety
of gifts given to us by God—a world where the resources of
the earth are used wisely and shared so that everyone has
enough. It is a world that exists as "God's economy."

   Douglas Meeks suggests a new metaphor for God, the

metaphor of *Economist*. He bases his understanding on the word *economy* and its history of varied meanings and functions. He explores the Greek word *oikonomia* and conceives the idea of a household that would describe not only a family arrangement but also a global community. The world would be a place where the economy, politics, and power would create a just society.

> One of the most basic assumptions of modern economics is scarcity. . . . No matter how much society will be able to produce, it is claimed, there will always be scarcity. . . . The typical traditions uncover God as the Economist who constructs the household with a radically different assumption: *If* the righteousness of God is present, there is always enough to go around. From the manna in the desert, to Jesus' feeding of the multitudes, to the Lord's Supper, the biblical traditions depict the superabundance (*pleroma*) of God's Spirit as the starting point of God's household and its practice of hospitality.[3]

The creation stories in Genesis also tell of human rebellion that undermines the intended goodness of God's creation—sinfulness that attempts to reorder authority and control (Gen. 3:1–24). "A Brief Statement of Faith" of the Presbyterian Church (U.S.A.) makes the connection between the Genesis story (Gen. 3:8), human sinfulness, and what that means for "God's economy."

> In life and death we belong to God.
>> But we rebel against God; we hide from our Creator.
>>> Ignoring God's commandments,
>>> we violate the image of God in others and ourselves,
>>> accept lies as truth,
>>> exploit neighbor and nature,
>>> and threaten death to the planet entrusted to our care.[4]

A Brief Statement of Faith includes affirmations of God's grace and forgiveness, but an earlier statement by the Presbyterian Church speaks more directly to justice and economic issues. The Confession of 1967 is based on the concept of reconciliation and describes our world of contrasting wealth and poverty and the call to follow the example of Jesus Christ.

> The reconciliation of [humanity] through Jesus Christ makes it plain that enslaving poverty in a world of abundance is an intolerable violation of God's good creation. Because Jesus identified himself with the needy and exploited, the cause of the world's poor is the cause of his disciples. The church cannot condone poverty, whether it is the product of unjust social structures, exploitation of the defenseless, lack of natural resources, absence of technological understanding, or rapid expansion of populations. The church calls every [one] to use his [or her] abilities, his [or her] possessions, and the fruits of technology as gifts entrusted to him [or her] by God for the maintenance of his [or her] family and the advancement of the common welfare.[5]

Our response to God for the gifts of creation and for grace, forgiveness, and reconciliation in our relationships with God and one another is gratitude. Just as we cannot *own* creation or any part of life, we cannot simply take without acknowledging the Creator and giving thanks. Gratitude is not only a part of our worship, it becomes our way of living.

B. A. Gerrish links grace and gratitude in his study of John Calvin. He determined that God's liberality and humanity's response of gratitude are "not only the theme of the Lord's Supper but a fundamental theme, perhaps the most fundamental theme of [Calvin's] entire system of theology."[6]

Grace and gratitude are the experience we share in the sacrament of the Lord's Supper. Then just as that experience in worship is to be a model of our oneness in Christ and of an economy in which there is always enough for everyone gathered around the Table, so do grace and gratitude become a way of living for all of life. Grace extends to others in appreciation for their gifts, encouraging and enabling them to discover and develop talents, ideas, and ambitions without personal jealousy or fear. Gratitude extends beyond thankfulness for things we have to what we share and what we can envision.

The question becomes, what can we offer to God in gratitude and thanksgiving other than our words and songs of praise, or our gestures of grace and gratitude toward others in God's name? Are the offerings of our money that we give in worship part of that response? Are they really ours to give? Do they represent more than a portion of what we have earned and saved? If everything comes from God, what can we give in return?

In an article titled "Presentation of the Gifts: Orthodox Insights for Western Liturgical Renewal," the author, Episcopal priest E. C. Miller, wrote about the offering made in worship as an "exchange of gifts" with God. Much of what he had to say was based on the writing of a Romanian Orthodox priest Dumitru Staniloae and his "theology of gift." A gift is, to use Miller's words, "a dynamic process of personal interaction, expression, even surrender" in the "dialogue of

---

The Offering

A LESSON ABOUT THE MEANING
OF THE OFFERING IN WORSHIP

Session Plan 2

PURPOSE   The purpose of this study is to examine and reflect on the beliefs implicit in the routine practice of receiving an offering as part of worship. The discussion is meant to encourage sharing among participants about their habits, assumptions, and intentions for giving in order to grow in faith and practices of stewardship.

the gift."[7] Gift implies reciprocity: God gives the world with us as a part of it; we are bound together with all creation. We, in return, offer our gifts to God.

However, when the gifts of God, of and to the world, are truly understood, we are left with a dilemma: What could we possibly offer to God that does not already belong to God? Staniloae suggests that it is our creativity and imagination along with our freedom (also gifts from God) that allow us to make something new to offer back to God.

> [T]he gifts given to us by God can become our gifts to God through the fact that we are free to give things to God. We transform things into our gifts by the exercise of our freedom and by the love which we show to God. Toward this end, we are able to transform and combine them endlessly. God has given the world to humanity not only as a gift of continuous fruitfulness, but as one immensely rich in possible alterations, actualized by each person through individual freedom and labor. This actualization, like the multiplication of talents given by God, is humanity's gift to God.[8]

Can we create something new out of what God has given us? Something God did not create? Staniloae's work is helpful in thinking through the paradox of giving gifts to God, whether in the Sunday morning offering or in any other gesture. God may be like a parent who tries to provide every benefit and advantage for a child, and then is surprised and delighted by the directions in which the child chooses to use those gifts, ways not imagined by the parent while the child was growing up.

> In gratitude to God, empowered by the Spirit,
>   we strive to serve Christ in our daily tasks
>   and to live holy and joyful lives,
>   even as we watch for God's new heaven and new earth,
>   praying, "Come, Lord Jesus!"[9]

Money, wealth, possessions, and faith—these gifts of creation from the Creator may, in the end, be best understood in very simple terms. When we give a gift to someone else, we expect certain things of the one who receives our gift. First, we expect them to say thank you. Then we hope that they will enjoy what we have chosen to give them. We want them to take care of it so that they can enjoy it for a long time; and we want to be remembered for having given it to them. We want them to find ways of using our gift so that it won't be put away where it might spoil or rust, break down, or get broken. And we hope that they will share our gift with others who also might find joy in it.

Say thank you. Use it. Take care of it, and share it.

> All your works shall give thanks to you, O LORD,
>   and all your faithful shall bless you.
> They shall speak of the glory of your kingdom,
>   and tell of your power,
> to make known to all people
>   your mighty deeds,
> and the glorious splendor of your kingdom.
>
> You open your hand,
>   satisfying the desire of every living thing.
>
> My mouth will speak the praise of the LORD,
>   and all flesh will bless his holy name forever and ever.
>   Ps. 145:10–12, 16, 21

NOTES

1. John Calvin, *Institutes of the Christian Religion*, 3.7.1; ed. John T. McNeill, tr. Ford Lewis Battles (Philadelphia: Westminster Press, 1960).

2. The Heidelberg Catechism, 4.026, *Book of Confessions* (*The Constitution*, Part I, Presbyterian Church (U.S.A.); Louisville, Ky.: Office of the General Assembly, 1999), 4.026. Hereafter: *Book of Confessions*, PC(USA).

3. M. Douglas Meeks, *God the Economist: The Doctrine of God and Political Economy* (Minneapolis: Fortress Press, 1989), 12.

28   The Price of Faith

4. A Brief Statement of Faith, lines 33–38, *Book of Confessions*, PC(USA).

5. The Confession of 1967, *Book of Confessions*, PC(USA).

6. B. A. Gerrish, *The Eucharistic Theology of John Calvin: Grace and Gratitude* (Minneapolis: Fortress Press, 1993), 20.

7. E. C. Miller Jr., "Presentation of the Gifts: Orthodox Insights for Western Liturgical Renewal," *Worship* 60, no. 1 (January 1986): 27.

8. Ibid., 29–30.

9. A Brief Statement of Faith, lines 72–76.

Chapter 5

Trust and Hope

> *Do not store up for yourselves treasures on earth, where moth and rust consume and where thieves break in and steal; but store up for yourselves treasures in heaven, where neither moth nor rust consumes and where thieves do not break in and steal. For where your treasure is, there your heart will be also.*
>
> *The eye is the lamp of the body. So, if your eye is healthy, your whole body will be full of light; but if your eye is unhealthy, your whole body will be full of darkness. If then the light in you is darkness, how great is the darkness!*
>
> *No one can serve two masters; for a slave will either hate the one and love the love the other, or be devoted to the one and despise the other. You cannot serve God and wealth.*
>
> —Matthew 6:19–24

*T*he witness of our faith in the sovereignty of God may be seen in what we do and what we say about the one whom we trust and in whom we hope—or in *what* we trust and hope. Money has power in North American society. Money is a means of exchange for work done or for food and other necessities purchased. It has value, and we trust that our money will hold its value over time so that our earning, spending, and saving will in some way ensure food for tomorrow and for the rest of our life. The economic system is built on the unspoken agreement that we trust the system enough that we are willing to contribute to it and build our daily lives around it.

Where Your Treasure Is

A BIBLE STUDY ABOUT
PRIORITIES IN DAILY LIVING
BASED ON MATTHEW 6:19–24

Session Plan 3

PURPOSE   This Bible study deals with the things we have and the priorities we choose in life. It is intended to encourage a thoughtful discussion of beliefs and practices concerning issues of consumption, the use of time and money, lifestyle, and the values and goals of individuals and congregations.

Money is a necessity in our society. If we could simply isolate it as a means of bartering—giving what we have in order to get what we need—money would be just a useful tool. But money represents more than the value printed or stamped on our bills and coins. The dollars and pennies have *relative* value, and that relative value transfers to whatever or whomever it is attached.

Price tags at the grocery store or shopping mall are clear examples of the relative value of what we need and/or desire. But what that value is—the price—is determined by a complex system of supply and demand, beauty and fashion, desire for comfort and security, and the role of advertising, among other factors.

The relative value of money is also seen in the compensation for and social recognition of the work we do. Money, in some sense, becomes a measure of our personal value as seen by others and ourselves. Our worth becomes wrapped up in what society is willing to pay for the gifts we have and how we use them in our choice of vocation. The value of who we are is seen in what we choose to purchase, where we choose to live—and whether or not we have enough money to have choices.

The questions of faith emerge at the line between money as a means to function and to do good, and money as a measure of value and worth according to our culture of consumers. These questions are matters of faith and trust, and by extension, a matter of hope for the future.

Value and worth, for Christians, are not to be decided by monetary measures, but by faith in God's purpose for our world and the ultimate goodness of creation. As we live in the world and depend on money for life and livelihood, we need to put money and all related issues into the context of faith. We cannot separate faith and money.

Although the Theological Declaration of Barmen was written during the time of Hitler's Germany in the 1930s, at issue was the sovereignty of God and the authority of Christ over all aspects of life. For that time, the question concerned government, but the same affirmation of faith applies to money, wealth, and possessions.

> We reject the false doctrine, as though there were areas of our life in which we would not belong to Jesus Christ, but to other lords—areas in which we would not need justification and sanctification through him.[1]

Money, the values we attribute to it, and the judgments we make in using it must have integrity with the rest of our convictions and statements of faith. The church, by virtue of its call to live in "God's economy," must be countercultural. Douglas Oldenburg, when he was president of Columbia Theological Seminary, was asked to give his theological reflection in response to the results of research done by Dean Hoge and group, and by Sylvia and John Ronsvalle. His address was given at conferences sponsored by the Presbyterian Church (U.S.A.) in 1995.

> The church has failed to be a counter-cultural community, creating a community where people have different values than the surrounding culture. . . . It is obvious to all of us that our culture places a premium value on consuming, buying more and more, immediate gratification, materialism, and believing that more is always better. Our economic system depends on people sharing those values, and the advertising industry feeds them by constantly bombarding us with such seductive messages. Our economic credo is that greater joy and security in life come from making more and more money and buying more and more things. It's a powerful force, almost irresistible, and all of us are seduced by it. To one degree or another we have all bought into it and so have the people in our congregations.[2]

The Sermon on the Mount makes our choice simple—we can serve God or wealth. Again, it is not about money as such, but about accumulating money and the values we attach to money, or the values we allow money to give to people, places, and things.

In Matthew 6, just before the choice between God and wealth is presented to us, verses 22 and 23 offer insight on our values and how they affect the well-being of our whole body, that is, our entire life. The following is from Clarence Jordan's *Cotton Patch Version* of the Gospel, with his commentary:

> *The body depends on the eyes for light. Now if your eyes are in focus, then the body will have clear light. But if your eyes are not in focus, then your whole body will be in confused darkness.*
>
> Your sense of values is to the soul what the eye is to the body. It enables you to see things in their proper perspec-

tive. It enables you to get your bearings and a sense of direction. But the eye must be in focus. If both eyes are fastened on a single objective, then you are seeing clearly—you are not confused. But if your eye is out of focus from attempting to look at more than one object at a time, your "light" will be darkness; you will see nothing clearly.[3]

We must make a choice. We cannot adopt God's ways *and* the ways of the world, Christian values and consumer values—we cannot serve God and *mammon*. Douglas Hare in his commentary has observed that we try to do both.

> Not with our minds but with our lives we have treated Matt. 6:24 as if it were a parallel to 22:21: "Render to mammon the things that are mammon's, and to God the things that are God's." To God belongs one hour on Sunday. Mammon gets the rest![4]

Faith is a matter of trust. In A Brief Statement of Faith, we repeat again and again that our trust is in the one triune God: "We trust in Jesus Christ . . . , We trust in God . . . , We trust in God the Holy Spirit." That trust is held in the present and for the future. The Sermon on the Mount continues in 6:25–33 with words of assurance and a lesson about trust.

> Do not worry about your life, what you will eat or what you will drink, or about your body, what you will wear. . . . Indeed your heavenly Father knows that you need all these things.

By itself, this text is a good reminder that life is more than what we eat and drink or wear; and that God values us. But its place in the Gospel, immediately after the insistent lesson that "You cannot serve God and wealth," makes clear the connections between money, possessions, wealth, and faith. We *cannot trust* money for the present or the future.

Society expects us to do just that, however. We have banks and trust companies; we invest in the futures market; and we purchase insurance to protect ourselves, our possessions, and even our ability to work and earn money. Again we are faced with the choice between money as a means of functioning in society and money as the ultimate end of our trust.

What or whom we trust not only affects daily living but also determines what we expect of the future. We begin to imagine the world as it might be according to the best of what we think has value. In turn, what we hope for the future impacts the way we live in the present. If "God's economy," in which everyone is worthy and everyone has enough, is what we imagine for the future, then we will find ways to bring that world about if only in small ways.

Elsa Tamez, president of the Biblical Seminary of Latin America in Costa Rica, offers a third-world perspective on the present times of unequal wealth and the global economy. Using the Old Testament book of Ecclesiastes, she finds several clues for survival and understanding. One of these is an affirmation of the life of eating, drinking, and finding pleasure in work.

> When the logic of society is to produce in the least time possible because time is money, Qohelet invites us to live the time of eternity within the history of short and measured time. And we can only experience this time of eternity when we enjoy life with the community with which we share it. . . . This is not a joy that turns its back indifferently to the dehumanization of our time, nor is it the product of a cynical helplessness in the face of those excluded from economic policies. . . . It has to do with mocking death by holding on to life. It has to do with living by the logic of God's grace, thus challenging the logic of the dehumanizing law of profit that knows no mercy.[5]

As part of the first-world consumer culture, we need to hear Tamez's words and understand our responsibility in the global economy. One statement she makes reinforces the idea of the future's bearing on the present and has implications for our role in bringing about a world where money, wealth, and possessions are shared: "We must live life as if it were eternal."

The future as God has promised, therefore, is not something for which we idly wait, rather, what we work toward now. We can trust in God to fulfill the promise; we can invest ourselves because we not only hope but also trust. Marjorie Suchocki describes this faith in terms of process theology.

> God is the future of the world in two senses. First, God offers the world its immediate future in history through every moment of its becoming. But second, God is the destiny of all the world beyond history. . . . [S]uch a God offers hope.[6]

Our hope cannot be in the money values of society—they cannot be depended on to be just and fair; they shift too easily; and they are determined not by God's word and God's purpose but by human self-interest. We are called to live by faith, a faith that is evident in all aspects of our lives—worship, prayer, church attendance, bank accounts, and habits of spending, saving and sharing our money, wealth, and possessions.

We trust in God the Holy Spirit,
    Everywhere the giver and renewer of life.
In a broken and fearful world
the Spirit gives us courage
    to pray without ceasing,
    to witness among all peoples to Christ as Lord and Savior,
    to unmask idolatries in Church and culture,
    to hear the voices of peoples long silenced,
    and to work with others for justice, freedom, and peace . . .
as we watch for God's new heaven and new earth. . . .[7]

NOTES

1. Theological Declaration of Barmen, *Book of Confessions*, PC(USA), 8.15.

2. Douglas W. Oldenburg, "Theological Reflection," Research Conference on Giving, Presbyterian Church (U.S.A.), Atlanta, August 1995.

3. Clarence Jordan, *Sermon on the Mount*, rev. ed. (Valley Forge, Pa.: Judson Press, 1952), 92.

4. Douglas R. A. Hare, *Matthew,* Interpretation: A Bible Commentary for Teaching and Preaching (Louisville, Ky.: John Knox Press, 1993), 73.

5. Elsa Tamez, "Of Silence and Cries: Job and Qohelet in the 90s," The Caldwell Lectures, Louisville Presbyterian Theological Seminary, February 2–4, 1998.

6. Marjorie Hewitt Suchocki, *God, Christ, Church: A Practical Guide to Process Theology*, rev. ed. (New York: Crossroad, 1992), 36.

7. A Brief Statement of Faith, lines 52–53, 65–71, 75.

Chapter 6

Managing Money

> *Take care! Be on your guard against all kinds*
> *of greed; for one's life does not consist in the*
> *abundance of possessions.*
> *"You fool! This very night your life is being*
> *demanded of you. And the things you have pre-*
> *pared, whose will they be?" So it is with those*
> *who store up treasures for themselves but are*
> *not rich toward God.*
> —Luke 12:15, 20–21

*I*ncluded with stewardship education materials for children produced by the Presbyterian Church (U.S.A.) is a money bank with three partitions labeled "spending," "saving," and "offering." Teaching children how to manage money seems simple. There are only so many things that can be done—we can buy something, we can put it away temporarily to save it for something we might want or need later, or we can give it to someone else. The three slots on top of the children's bank make the lesson clear, objective, and concrete.

For adults, the choices may be just as simple, but the issues are much more complex. The Bible offers general guidelines against greed, covetousness, and false gain and teaches us instead to put Christ first in our lives and to be "rich toward God." But without specific instruction about how to manage our money, we are left with questions about exactly what it means to live faithfully. Added to the children's decisions of what to spend, save, and give of our money is the question of how we earn it. Matters of faith include all of these decisions about how we get money and what we do with the money we get.

Our attitudes and patterns and our habits and practices in dealing with money are more often developed from observation and expectation. We learn from parents, other family members, friends, and society in general. We learn from them, and then either follow their example or make a point of doing something different. In choosing what we do to earn money and in deciding how to spend, save, or give it away, we make plans to avoid financial disaster or to secure a comfortable living. By default, we learn almost entirely by experience rather than from intentional teaching by the church or other individuals and communities of faith.

An Autobiography about Money

A PERSONAL HISTORY OF PRACTICES AND ATTITUDES

Session Plan 4

PURPOSE This lesson is intended to raise our awareness of the people and experiences that have affected our practices, habits, and attitudes about money and to reflect on the continuing significance these have as we deal particularly with issues of giving to people, causes, and the church.

As noted earlier, there is a general reluctance to talk about money and faith. Whether we Christians are at church, at home, with friends, in public, or in private conversations, we are not likely to talk about our money decisions or concerns.

We can find biblical lessons to help us, however—lessons to study and wrestle with for ourselves individually and for us together as a community of faith. Some of these are the New Testament parables of Jesus. The parables are helpful because they draw us toward life as it might be. Jesus used experiences and subjects from ordinary life, but his purpose was not to reinforce what already existed. Rather, these parables were used to spark the imagination so that those who heard might begin to live in new ways and work toward a new reality according to God's purpose.

In her book *Metaphorical Theology: Models of God in Religious Language*, Sallie McFague speaks of parables as metaphors, and she understands parables not only as the lessons Jesus taught, but the parables as Jesus himself.

> What must always be kept in mind is that the parables as metaphors and the life of Jesus as a metaphor of God provide characteristics for theology: a theology guided by them is open-ended, tentative, indirect, tensive, iconoclastic, transformative. . . . The many parables of the kingdom tell us something about the rule of God, of what it means to live in the world according to God's way.[1]

The parables are especially pertinent to the discussion of faith and money because they are open-ended and because they continue to speak to us, allowing and requiring us to struggle with their meaning for us. The parables leave us to work out the details—they lead us to imagine what life would be if it were God's kind of world, but then we are given responsibility to translate that into personal and corporate life and our own decisions.

The parable of the Pounds in Luke 19:11–27 (similar to Matthew 25:14–30) teaches us that we are given gifts to use in ways that produce something more than we first had; and more than that, something that is good and beneficial. Sharon Ringe in her commentary on this text sees eschatological implications.

> The allegorical equivalents are clear: After the crucifixion and resurrection, Jesus leaves the disciples and ascends to sit at God's right hand. In the meantime, until his return at the final judgment, Jesus has entrusted his followers to carry on his ministry and to make it "prosper" and grow into the mission of the church. At an appropriate time, the risen Christ will return to demand an account of what they have done with the responsibility entrusted to them.[2]

The same lesson can be seen in the parable of the Fig Tree (Luke 13:6–9), that there is a purpose for every part of creation. And while some things and some people may require more tending and attention, they are worth nurturing so they can bear fruit.

The matters of greed, selfishness, anxiety, and wanting the power to control and secure the future are the subjects of the parable of the rich fool (Luke 12:13–21) who tries to save too much. He operates in a society that measures success by how much is accumulated, so he builds bigger barns to store his grain and all his goods—much as we do with overstuffed attics, basements, and rented storage space.

One parable that has always been difficult to fully understand is the parable of the Dishonest Manager (or shrewd manager or dishonest steward) found in Luke 16:1–13, and it is particularly relevant to questions about how we manage money and what "God's economy" might be like. Ringe's comments help us understand this parable, too.

> The key is in the manager's identification by the owner as a "manager of injustice" (16:8a), and in the subsequent identification of wealth, not as "dishonest," but as "wealth of injustice" (16:9). The underlying assumption is of an economy of scarcity, where the quantity of wealth avail-

able is fixed. Some have more only if others have less. . . .
By reducing the amount owed by the (obviously poorer)
debtors to the rich man, the manager is doing justice—a
way of doing his job as a "manager of injustice" that no
longer aims at perpetuating and even adding to old
inequities, but instead reflects the new "economy" of
which Jesus is the herald.[3]

Ringe goes on to say that this parable offers a model for leadership and management that doesn't require a lifestyle of
poverty but challenges us to manage wealth in ways that are
just. In doing so, we create new communities where the accu-
mulation of wealth is not the goal. Instead the wealth is distributed so that all may share the benefits.

Is this applicable in our world? Do we have situations like
this? In some ways the "dishonest manager" is analogous to
a modern-day business manager of a company owned by a
larger parent company who has decided to sell out to yet
another larger company. The business manager has an opportunity before the buyout is announced to make some decisions that may not benefit the holding company but would be
beneficial to the smaller company's employees. What is the
right thing to do?

The question of what is "right" appears again and again in
a chapter written by Sharon Parks in a book titled *Practicing
Our Faith: A Way of Life for a Searching People*. She raises
issues about "right labor" and "right technology," searching
for what is good and just in our shared economy.[4] In the past,
efforts to find work that was right meant taking a stand against
slavery. Now it means looking for people in places where the
work is demeaning or causing hardship in order to satisfy our
comfort or pleasure, and then taking a stand against it and
working to create change. Right technology means asking
first such basic questions about how computers, television,
better forms of communication, home appliances, cars, and
such will affect our patterns of living and the whole of the

earth in order to use them beneficially. All of these issues raise
further questions about our choice of vocation.

In our current culture with its growing variety of occupa-
tions and specialties, are there some jobs that are not "right"?
If we understand our work as a calling or a ministry—and as
Christians that is our sense of who we are and what we do—
then are there places in the work world that are not appropriate for us? Can we be teachers, doctors, librarians, computer
programmers, factory workers, farmers, welders, artists, store
clerks or whatever else without considering anything but
what it promises of salary and benefits?

There are other factors to help us decide whether or not a
job is "right." One is *where* our work is to be done—whether
we are working in a factory that produces cars or weapons;
whether we are programming computers for a hospital or the
state lottery. Whether any of these situations is right or wrong
must be decided, but the question is part of what we must
consider when choosing our vocation.

Another set of criteria to factor into our decision has to do
with what we find joy in doing and how that fits the world's
needs. Frederick Buechner gives this definition of vocation:

> There are all kinds of voices calling you to all different
> kinds of work, and the problem is to find out which is the
> voice of God rather than of society, say, or the superego,
> or self-interest.
>
> By and large a good rule for finding out is this. The kind
> of work God usually calls you to is the kind of work (a)
> that you need to do and (b) that the world most needs to
> have done. . . .
>
> Neither the hair shirt nor the soft berth will do. The
> place God calls you is the place where your deep gladness
> and the world's deep hunger meet.[5]

These are all matters of stewardship—using the talents,
resources, and opportunities God has given us as gifts, and

matching them to what needs to be done in the world. The choice we make is important not only in terms of our work, but also because we are teaching others by our example.

How we earn money, even how much we earn, has to do with whether we think of money as a means or an end and how we manage it or allow it to manage our lives. There are demands and expectations from others as well as from ourselves for spending, saving, and earning more. Some of these are very real responsibilities, such as providing basic necessities, long-term care, or education. Some are only imagined needs. Often the real or the imagined needs lead us to search for one job after another that promises to pay more. For some people, the problem is low-paying work that forces them to work longer hours or to have more than one job. For others, it is only the desire to have more, as our society seems to encourage.

> We are working more and faster, in part because the incentive structures in our present economy have a bias toward either long work hours or multiple part-time jobs. We work at these jobs to secure our sense of belonging and well-being, increasingly defined by access to the goods and services we need and want.
>
> One consequence is what early Quakers called "cumber." Billions of marketing dollars are spent worldwide to make a dazzling array of products and services attractive, even "necessary." Moreover, the market has become ubiquitous. . . .
>
> The consequent cumber affects our ways of life. The stuff we accumulate requires our energy and attention to secure, maintain, and finally discard, and the pervasive advertising-entertainment images of a consumer culture lodge in our souls, shaping our desires and agendas.[6]

The pervasive desire for having more and more, requiring more and more money and more and more work continues to spread in our culture. Tom Tewell has called it a disease.

These are some questions for diagnosis: Is bill-paying time at your home ever stressful for you and the members of your family? Have you ever compared what you have with what other people have? Have you ever equated your value as a person with what you earn or with what you own? Do you sometimes go shopping to buy clothing or some other tangible item to make you feel better after a setback or disappointment? Do you ever lose sleep worrying about how you're going to finance a college education, how you're going to care for aging parents, or how you're going to pay all the bills?

If you answered "yes" to any of those questions, you may be sicker than you thought. You may have that dreaded virus, *philargyria* [the love of money].[7]

Sharon Parks speaks again in terms of what is "right."

The practice of simplicity is an orientation to life that can, over time, foster a sense of right proportion and right relation within the dynamic and interdependent household of the whole earth community.[8]

Faith and Money

A BIBLE STUDY ABOUT WORK,
EARNINGS, AND STEWARDSHIP
BASED ON JAMES 2:14–18

Session Plan 5

PURPOSE   The purpose of this study is to examine the connections between what we do and say and what we believe. By hearing the Scripture text from the New Testament book of James read in new ways, we may discover a fuller understanding of the meaning and practice of faithful Christian stewardship.

Simplicity in our personal lifestyle has the potential for relieving the hurried pace and the anxieties about earning enough, accumulating too much, spending money to take care of our "stuff" and having money to give away. However, finding ways to simplify our lives is not the only or the complete answer to questions about managing money. We are part of a complex economic society that has become global. Simple purchases of necessities can affect the survival and livelihood of people in other nations. Our financial responsibilities often extend across generations within our families.

The answers do not come easily. We need one another to help make sense of our world and our place as Christians in it. Together we may discern what the Bible has to teach us and what the implications are for each one of us. To do so requires wisdom and trust.

In some instances we have begun to examine our financial practices for what is just and right. Many denominations have set policies that prohibit moneys from being invested in corporations that do business in countries where human rights are violated, or in companies that have made decisions that are ethically questionable. Some congregations and individuals have followed this example. The challenge is for us to explore *all* aspects of our money, work, savings, and giving in light of biblical teaching, and to create opportunities for discussion within the life of the church.

NOTES

1. Sallie McFague, *Metaphorical Theology: Models of God in Religious Language* (Philadelphia: Fortress Press), 19.

2. Sharon H. Ringe, *Luke*, Westminster Bible Companion (Louisville, Ky.: Westminster John Knox Press, 1995), 235.

3. Ibid., 214.

4. Sharon Daloz Parks, "Household Economics," in *Practicing Our Faith,* ed. Dorothy C. Bass, 53–56.

5. Frederick Buechner, *Wishful Thinking: A Theological ABC* (New York: Harper & Row, 1973), 95.

6. Parks, 45–46.

7. Thomas K. Tewell, "A Spreading Spiritual Virus," *Stewardship 1995—Part Two,* Stewardship Education, Presbyterian Church (U.S.A.), 15.

8. Parks, 50.

Chapter 7

Giving and Asking

*The point is this: the one who sows sparingly
will also reap sparingly, and the one who sows
bountifully will also reap bountifully. Each of
you must give as you have made up your mind,
not reluctantly or under compulsion, for God
loves a cheerful giver. And God is able to provide you with every blessing in abundance, so
that by always having enough of everything,
you may share abundantly in every good work.*

*Through the testing of this ministry you glo-
rify God by your obedience to the confession of
the gospel of Christ and by the generosity of your
sharing with them and with all others, while they
long for you and pray for you because of the sur-
passing grace of God that he has given you.
Thanks be to God for his indescribable gift!*
—2 Corinthians 9:6–8, 13–15

*A minister wrote to a wealthy and influential
individual in the community to request a donation to a worthy charity and soon received a
curt refusal which ended, "As far as I can see,
this Christian business is just one continuous
Give, give, give." Replied the minister, "I wish
to thank you for the best definition of the Christian life I have yet heard."*
—*The World Treasury of Religious Quotations*,
ed. Ralph L. Woods

Asking and giving are part of handling money—as we earn, spend, and share it, and as we participate in the financial life of the church and society in general. But asking and giving, and the ways in which we do them, also say something about our relationships with God and others. Our readiness to give

---

Spare Change

AN EXERCISE IN ASKING AND GIVING

Session Plan 6

PURPOSE   The purpose of this exercise has many dimensions. As an introductory activity, it helps participants begin to consider the subject of stewardship in a concrete and personal way, and it serves to acquaint the participants with one another. At another level, the exercise raises issues of personal and societal attitudes about the value of money, how needs can be met by giving money, and the ways in which wealth is distributed. At yet another level, the exercise points to theological beliefs that are reflected in our behavior and our beliefs about community, responsibility, charity, and stewardship.

---

money and the amount we are willing to give depend upon who is asking, the purpose for which they are asking, and our own motives. When asked by a member of our family to contribute to a gift for another relative, we are generally willing to give. However, the request might be complicated by our feelings toward the intended recipient, which might make us more or less reluctant to give. We might also ask what is our fair share, thinking that the responsibility of giving should be divided equitably among family members.

Charity Begins at Home

A CASE STUDY ABOUT ATTITUDES AND
RELATIONSHIPS BETWEEN GIVERS
AND RECIPIENTS

Session Plan 7

PURPOSE   This case study examines the dynamics of changing attitudes and relationships within the community of the church when the recipients of mission giving become active members of the congregation. The study enables a discussion of motives, beliefs, and expectations of individuals and the congregation as a whole.

Our own participation in giving and asking carries a variety of motivations and attitudes about money, its value to us and others, and feelings about the people with whom we live. When, in 2 Corinthians 8 and 9, the apostle Paul asks the people to contribute to the church in Jerusalem, all of these dynamics are at work. It is a wonderful text that helps us to understand the roles of asker, giver, and recipient and the relationships among them. It is more than an example of successful fund-raising; it places asking and giving into a theological context and offers instruction for personal lifestyles as well as the shared life of the church.

> The words [Paul] used, so often translated as collection or offering, are larger, theological, spiritual words. In the fifth verse of chapter nine, the word is *eulogia*, blessing. It is translated as offering or gift, but it is the word for blessing. This effort of Paul's isn't just the mundane exchange of money; this is the giving of oneself as a blessing to those other Christians. . . .

> You give to help these people [in Jerusalem], not
> because of some duty but because God has bound all of
> you together in a fellowship of love. Blessing and praise
> and fellowship are all tied up and mixed up with the very
> earthy giving of money.[1]

This rich theological language is also noted by Jouette Bassler in her book *God and Mammon: Asking for Money in the New Testament*. She points to the importance of *koinonia* and the assumption Paul made that all members of Christ's church wherever they live belong to the same community. The word *charis*, meaning gift, favor, or grace, is used frequently throughout these chapters. She also points to *eulogia* (praise, blessing) and adds *diakonia* (ministry, service) and *leitourgia* (the work of the people, liturgy) to the list of terms that Paul used to put his asking into the context of faith. Thus giving becomes praise and blessing, a ministry and the work of the people.

> Not only are these terms abundant in these two chapters,
> but Paul often plays one term off another, or plays with
> different meanings of a term, always weaving them so
> deeply into his argument that the theological dimensions
> of his request cannot be disengaged from the request
> itself.[2]

Guidance and instruction for asking and giving may be found by simply working our way through 2 Corinthians 8 and 9. First, Paul's request is on behalf of others, not himself. Whether or not that someone is known by name, a need is apparent and a relationship is assumed. We are one community—the church, our neighborhood, our world—and because we are related, we will *want* to give, not *have* to give.

Paul appeals to the example set by the Macedonian church (8:2ff.), knowing that what others do offers encouragement and endorsement. He reminds the Corinthians that giving is first of all directed toward God (8:5), and that Christ serves as a model for true richness (8:9–10). In the following verses, it is explained that giving should not cause hardship. In this case it is just a matter of sharing between those who have and those who have not; there may be a time in the future when circumstances are reversed, and then they could expect to be helped as they are helping others (8:13–15). We are always partners in giving with the recipients and with those who take our gifts and minister in our name (8:23). Our giving is never individual, it is always joined to the giving of others, whether our gift is money, time, energy, or vision.

The first part of chapter 9 indicates that Paul was confident that the church members in Corinth would give generously. Perhaps this was an effort to put pressure on them, but it might also have been Paul's enthusiasm and commitment to what he believed was a worthwhile mission and his conviction that all followers of Christ are "in it" together.

Our reasons for giving may range from a sense of duty to mere habit. But Paul wants us to give cheerfully with thanks and praise to God (9:6–15). To give is to bless and be blessed. A reminder that God cares for us and our every need frees us to "share abundantly in every good work."

The Mission Front

A CASE STUDY ABOUT BUDGET DECISIONS OF A CHURCH SESSION

Session Plan 8

PURPOSE   This case study examines the dynamics of financial decision-making among congregational leaders. It raises questions about who initiates ideas that have an impact on the budget, the authority of the congregational governing board, the role of the pastor, and attitudes about local needs and worldwide mission.

We have become accustomed to the ways in which the
church asks for money: budgets are presented, mission causes
are endorsed. We use envelopes and offering plates, and ordi-
narily our giving is part of our worship. These practices,
however, developed over time, often out of cultural changes
and movements within the church and its structure, as well
as from theological convictions.

The *Westminster Directory* of 1644 was clear in its direction: "The Collection for the poore is so to be ordered, that
no part of the publique worship be thereby hindred."[3] Still,
the importance of serving the needs of the poor was always
understood to be part of Christian responsibility. Calvin
included the instruction to offer alms in his benediction at the
end of worship in order to make a clear connection between
the sacred world of worship in the sanctuary and the secular
world and its needs.

> The Lord bless thee, and keep thee; The Lord make . . .
> *Whereunto is added, to remind the people of the duty of
> alms-giving, as it is customary upon leaving the church,*
> Depart in peace. Remember the poor; and the God of
> peace be with you. Amen.[4]

The *Westminster Directory* was the guiding document for
Reformed churches in colonial America and was formally
adopted for the Presbyterian Church by the General Assembly in 1729 and reaffirmed in 1786. Generally, there were no
Sunday offerings as part of the worship during the seven-
teenth and eighteenth centuries, and all giving was voluntary.
Collections or subscriptions were made to support the local
church and minister. Special collections were taken for particular needs as they occurred. Gifts were made in money or
in kind.

Pew rents followed the practice of subscriptions, and this
new manner of collections lasted for more than a hundred and

fifty years. Church buildings at the time were constructed without seating, and gradually pews were added, with the first ones often reserved for the family of the minister. The practices varied with the congregation. In some places the pews were privately built and then sold when a family moved or the owner died. In other congregations, pews were constructed by the church and sold, rented, or assessed annually. Sometimes the pews would be assigned by committee regardless of the ability to pay, but preferred seating was always at the front of the sanctuary and the poor were relegated to the drafty back corners. As time passed, the practice of pew rental or ownership came under attack partly because some pews had become elaborate boxes with locks and keys and added luxuries of hassocks and cushions. Some saw the practice as an opportunity for profit.

> Four hundred dollars he had paid.
> He sold the pew for six, and made
> A handsome profit by the trade.
> The furniture he sold by lot,
> And more than what it cost he got.
> I do not say that there are any
> Who join the church to make a penny;
> But in a case like this, you see,
> A *pew* is not bad property.[5]

The nineteenth century saw the rapid development of benevolent organizations and auxiliary societies, so many that the General Assembly of the Presbyterian Church officially proclaimed, in 1819, that giving to them did not exempt a congregation from supporting General Assembly missions. Earlier, in 1804, the Presbyterian Church had to declare that one annual fund drive for mission would replace the numerous requests that came to the congregation from the General Assembly.

In the mid-1800s, collecting for benevolence became a

regular part of worship. In 1861 the General Assembly of the southern Presbyterian Church said that ministers should preach about giving frequently, parishioners should be taught regular, systematic giving, and elders should go house to house to solicit and encourage giving. Regular reports on giving should also be made to presbytery.

Although the first Presbyterian *Directory for Worship* was written and published in 1788, a chapter on the offering was not added until 1886. In that chapter, instructions were to train every member to give systematically and to view such offerings as "a solemn act of worship." The proper order of worship and the place of the offering in it, however, were left to the discretion of the minister and the session of the church. A year later, a system for soliciting individual pledges was endorsed.

The convergence of ideas and efforts to unify giving, promote pledging, and incorporate the offering of monetary gifts into meaningful worship gradually developed as other practices of raising necessary funds for the church were abused or taken to extremes. Church fairs, bazaars, lotteries, cakewalks, and such were getting out of hand, according to some, and giving in worship was not being given its proper context and understanding as an expression of gratitude and a means of grace.

The early twentieth century was also the time of "The Minister's Social Helper," a column in the *Ladies' Home Journal*. Women were encouraged to work for the church, and a number of innovative ideas were suggested: the talent plan where everyone *takes* a dollar from the offering plate and returns it with interest a few months later; commission selling; and collecting old goods to sell to junk dealers with all the returns given to the church.

Other methods for raising money were "The Lord's Acre," the "Church Farm," and "The Lord's Hour." In each case, the income from the property or the time in the workday was to be given to the church—in addition to tithing and regular offerings. Stories of the special bounty that came from these designated gifts were told for inspiration. There was a cranberry bog in New England in which the poorest acre (at the minister's request) was set aside as the Lord's acre, and only it among all the other surrounding acres survived the summer drought and an early frost to produce a yield greater than ever before.

Tithing gained renewed emphasis at this time, too. Again, stories of personal benefit and resulting financial success for those who tithed were spread as proof that this was a good method and a faithful practice for Christians. Pamphlets were written, testimonies were given, and congregations as a whole made efforts to encourage tithing, especially as the country prospered.

The changes in practices of giving are reflected in the differences among Presbyterian service books from 1906 to 1993. Although the offering was identified as an "act of worship" in the 1886 Directory for Worship, that designation did not appear in a service book until 1932. After that it was not mentioned at all, presumably because the offering was assumed to be an act of worship.

Other differences include the place of the offering in the order of worship and the type of prayer offered along with receiving the offering. According to the 1906 and 1932 service books, the offering was to be taken *after* the general prayer and *before* the sermon. In the 1946 book, it was before *or* after the sermon. By 1970 the offering was to be *after* the sermon and before the invitation to the Lord's Supper; this same instruction was given in 1993.

The different types of prayer at the time of the offering may help to explain the changes in the order of worship. In 1906 the prayer was for God's blessing, and in 1932 and 1946 it was a prayer of dedication. In 1970 it was called a prayer of thanksgiving. When the offering follows the Scripture and sermon—hearing God's Word—the appropriate response is one of thanks. When the offering is placed earlier in the service, prayers of dedication and petition for blessing seem more fitting. All three attitudes—of asking for God's blessing, dedicating ourselves and our gifts, and thanking God—are consistent with the meaning of the offering and our different reasons for giving.

The Sunday Morning Offering

A HISTORY AND STUDY OF THE PLACE
OF THE OFFERING IN WORSHIP

Session Plan 9

PURPOSE   The purpose of this lesson is to examine the ways in which the offering is received as part of Sunday morning worship. By looking at what the practices have been in the past and what they are in the present, participants will explore the theological meanings and implications of the different ways.

From our look at Scripture and the history of our practices of giving in the church, we find some guidance along with clues to the right questions about asking and giving. We learn that it is done within a community with a sense of partnership, whether the community is small or large, and whether it is nearby or far away. "People give to people" is more than a successful financial campaign strategy.[6] It signifies the relationships assumed and implied when people share resources with one another.

The gifts of who we are and what we have are given to us by God to manage and use, to care for and share. They are ours to enjoy and offer to others cheerfully as a gesture of our inexpressible gratitude to God.

Note: Although some of the references in this chapter are particularly Presbyterian, others are more general and may be similar to the experience of other Protestant denominations. Reading other church documents or referring to church history books may be helpful in seeing the relation of this material to churches other than Presbyterian.

NOTES

1. Isabel W. Rogers, "Stewardship and the Gifts of God," *Stewardship 1995—Part One*, Stewardship Education, Presbyterian Church (U.S.A.), 27.

2. Jouette M. Bassler, *God and Mammon:Asking for Money in the New Testament* (Nashville: Abingdon Press, 1991), 101.

3. *Commonwealth Service Book*: A Directory for the Publique Worship of God throughout the Three Kingdoms of England, Scotland, and Ireland; together with an Ordinance of Parliament for the taking away of the *Book of Common Prayer* (1644).

4. Charles W. Baird, *The Presbyterian Liturgies, Historical Sketches* (Grand Rapids: Baker Book House, 1960), 44. The first edition was titled *Eutaxia, or the Presbyterian Liturgies* (New York: M. W. Dodd, 1855). The second edition, upon which the 1960 volume is based, was published in London in 1856.

5. Luther P. Powell, *Money and the Church* (New York: Association Press, 1962), 132.

6. Kennon L. Callahan, *Giving and Stewardship in an Effective Church* (San Francisco: HarperSanFrancisco, 1992), 35.

Chapter 8

The Household of God

> *So then you are no longer strangers and aliens,
> but you are citizens with the saints and also
> members of the household of God, built upon
> the foundation of the apostles and prophets,
> with Christ Jesus himself as the cornerstone.
> In him the whole structure is joined together
> and grows into a holy temple in the Lord; in
> whom you also are built together spiritually
> into a dwelling place for God.*
> —Ephesians 2:19–22

*C*reator and creation, trust and hope, managing money, and giving and asking are all categories of stewardship for biblical study and theological reflection; and they all have implications for and are understood most fully only within the community of the people of God. The metaphor of a "household" helps to describe relationships and responsibilities within the community. It is a metaphor that has been used by many people in recent years instead of the "kingdom" or "realm" of God.

Letty Russell, in her book *Household of Freedom: Authority in Feminist Theology*, proposed, as an alternative metaphor, "a new image of kingdom as love and community."

> If we were to pray "For thine is the *household* and the power and glory," this might convey to us that God's power and glory are to be seen not in domination but in the daily housekeeping of God's world.[1]

Douglas Meeks has also used the metaphor of household, which he bases on a translation of the Greek words related to stewardship.

> The Greek word from which we derive *economy*, *oikono-mia*, is a compound of *oikos*, household, and *nomos*, law or management. *Economy* means literally "the law or the management of the household." Household is connected with the production, distribution, and consumption of the necessities of life. . . . In an attenuated sense, then, we shall refer to whole economies as household. Without household people will not survive, for household is the mediation of what it takes to live.[2]

We must live with an awareness of our oneness as a world, a household, created by God. We must acknowledge our relationship to one another and to all creation for survival and for what is good and right. For our individualistic culture, this understanding of the common life is a difficult and radical outlook to adopt. It is not a pragmatic solution, but a theological stance.

Based on his reading of Jürgen Moltmann, "The Social Understanding of the Trinity," Meeks presents a description of God's unity that we should model in our life as a community.

> A critical doctrine of God . . . should show that God is not a radical individual but rather a community of diverse persons that finds unity in self-giving love rather than in substantialist or subjectivist principles of identity.
>
> The "mutual coinherence" of the persons of the Trinity is a model of interrelationships of the members of the household that God intends. All the persons of the triune

community have their own characteristics and their own tasks. Yet they are constituted as persons precisely by their relationships with the other persons of the community. The same should be said for the human economic community.[3]

For us, then, the meaning is that we find our individuality only within relationships, and these relationships happen only when we are together. Moreover, just as we understand God's "unity in self-giving love," so we will find our oneness in community as we too offer self-giving love.

Where Do You Stand?

AN EXERCISE COMPARING IDEAS AND ATTITUDES ABOUT STEWARDSHIP

Session Plan 10

PURPOSE   This activity and planned discussion are intended to raise the awareness of congregational leaders about ideas and attitudes they hold concerning stewardship in the church. The similarities and differences discovered among clergy and laity will help develop a definition of stewardship and effective programs and practices of stewardship in the church.

The questions of stewardship that face us in the larger issues of the global economy and environment and the more common everyday decisions of survival and consumption are too complex and difficult to make alone. We need the wisdom of the community. As Sharon Parks says, we need to be "figuring it out together." We need to challenge one another to ask questions that call us to examine our lifestyles, perhaps even our vocations, the use of our time, and our habits of giving. We need to overcome our reluctance to talk about faith and money by claiming trust in God and one another. We need to renew or begin habits of joyful generosity and hospitality. We have a responsibility to learn and teach these practices of faith within the household of God—the church, our homes, the world.

> We trust in God the Holy Spirit,
>> everywhere the giver and renewer of life.
> The Spirit justifies us by grace through faith,
>> sets us free to accept ourselves and to love God
>> and neighbor,
>> and binds us together with all believers
> in the one body of Christ, the Church.[4]

NOTES

1. Letty Russell, *Household of Freedom: Authority in Feminist Theology* (Philadelphia: Westminster Press, 1987), 83.

2. M. Douglas Meeks, *God the Economist: The Doctrine of God and the Political Economy* (Minneapolis: Fortress Press, 1989), 3.

3. Ibid., 11–12.

4. A Brief Statement of Faith.

PART THREE   Stewardship Study

Session Plans for Stewardship Study

Introduction

To experience a true education about stewardship is to be changed in some way. What we knew before, what we used to think, and the way we used to live will be affected in some way by what we learn. Such learning is most likely to occur within a group of people, a community. For us, that community is the church.

There is vitality within a group that cannot be experienced alone. There is a spirit of wisdom and insight that comes from the collective memory, experience, and faith of the group. Beliefs, confessions, shared history, relationships, the personal search for meaning, and the mystery of God's presence combine to create a community where transformative teaching and learning may take place. The community of the church provides a place for dialogue, storytelling, imagination, and action, a place that is necessary as we shape our self-identity and self-understanding as individuals and as a community. We need to tell our own stories, hear ourselves tell them, and have others listen. We need the stories of others to know their experience and to interpret our own. It is part of the Christian community's role to provide opportunities and settings for such storytelling, reflection, and learning—along with the struggles, confessions, inspirations, and celebrations.

Many aspects of the life of the church provide opportunities for education. We learn about faith in worship as well as in church school. We are challenged and our ideas expand when we participate in mission. We grow in understanding ourselves and others, and our relationship with God, through conversations at committee meetings and gatherings for fellowship. Some educational opportunities are planned and some are not. Some allow for reflection and sharing what is learned, and some are less intentional.

The session plans created for the study of stewardship are meant for times when learning is scheduled, whether for Sunday morning church school, a weekday evening program, a retreat, or a committee meeting. Most of these opportunities last for approximately one hour, and so the sessions are planned for approximately that amount of time. Any of them could be expanded with a more in-depth look at the subject. A few ideas are suggested within the instructions for the lessons themselves.

Each of the session plans may be used independently and for a single occasion, but two, three, or more of them can be used together for a daylong retreat. The plans could also be used for a series of stewardship studies over a period of several months or more. The specific topics and educational approaches are varied and adaptable to many settings.

Some of the sessions are introductory in nature, explore the definition of stewardship, or ask participants to begin evaluating their own stewardship choices in life. Other sessions lead participants to study Scripture, delve into the decisions congregations face concerning stewardship, or reflect on their personal faith and spiritual life.

While every session plan depends on conversation and discussion, the approaches differ to accommodate preferred teaching and learning styles and to provide variety. The case studies require reading before discussion, and the discussion may be carried on in pairs of participants, small groups, or the group as a whole. There are other session plans, such as no. 7, "Spare Change," that begin with an activity requiring conversation and interaction before more serious discussion and reflection take place. The person or persons planning for education will need to choose the topics and approaches that are most appropriate and effective for their own situation.

Several of the session plans have material for participants to use. Some pages are worksheets and others are case studies or texts for reading and discussion. All of these are to be copied before class time, and enough should be made for every participant. In each case, the copy may be enlarged to fill an 8½-by-11 paper.

- Session 1, Bible-Based Stewardship—copy pages 71–72 front to back
- Session 2, The Offering—copy page 77
- Session 3, Where Your Treasure Is—copy page 81
- Session 5, Faith and Money—copy page 89
- Session 7, Charity Begins at Home—copy pages 97–100 front to back
- Session 8, The Mission Front—copy pages 104–107 front to back
- Session 9, The Sunday Offering—copy pages 112–113

Most of the session plans have suggestions for ways in which the lessons learned may be applied, either at the close of the session or at a later time. The context—an ecumenical retreat or a church school class, for example—will determine the best way to use the suggestions or it may stimulate other ideas. The experience participants bring to the group, and the roles and responsibilities they have in the church may also bring about innovative ways to apply what has been shared and learned. It is important to find some way to put learning into action if the experience is to become transforming.

1. Bible-Based Stewardship

READING THE BIBLE FROM
A STEWARDSHIP PERSPECTIVE

> PURPOSE   The subject of stewardship is found
> throughout the Bible in texts that deal with money,
> ownership, and possessions as well as texts where
> the subject is implicit or understood in a broader
> sense. This session begins with building a definition
> of stewardship that includes all aspects of life for
> which we are called to be stewards and caretakers.
> It is meant to be an exercise that leads to reading the
> whole Bible with an expectation of finding lessons
> about stewardship.

Introduction

When the word *stewardship* is used, especially in the church,
people most often associate it with money and only money.
And when biblical texts that deal with stewardship are
sought, the subject is broadened only a little to include time
and talents. This Bible workshop is intended to develop a
more general perspective toward stewardship that includes
all aspects of life and our responsibility as stewards for all the
gifts and opportunities given to us by God.

The approach is to look first at the Scripture texts and then
to think of stewardship. This is instead of looking for texts that
mention the word *stewardship* or searching for places where
we think there might be something said about money, gifts,
or other stewardship-related words. The intent is not only to
discover the many relevant texts, but also to develop a definition of stewardship that encompasses the whole of creation:
human life, the environment, personal and community life,
energy, ideas, intellect, money, and faith. Many more words
could be added to this list, and that is just what is expected to
come out of this study as a definition is constructed by the
group and applied to their reading of the Bible.

Preparing the Session

Read through the session and work through the information, biblical texts, and questions for yourself. Consider other responses that might come from the group participants in preparation for leading them. Create your own list of stewardship words and phrases.

The session will require about one hour, depending on the number of participants and the options you choose in leading the session. If there is time, conclude with a discussion of what is to be done with what has been learned and experienced. Possibilities include writing the liturgy for a worship service with a variety of Scripture texts or just phrases and portions of the texts forming prayers for the day, the call to worship, or a litany. Another use would be to take several texts, or more, and create a theme for your financial stewardship campaign—use a variety of texts to write postcards to members of the congregation during the campaign. Engage the youth or children in your congregation to illustrate the texts participants have chosen. You may want to give this some thought in advance in order to have examples to share with the group.

Leading the Session

1. Begin with asking the participants to introduce themselves by saying aloud their names and one of their favorite passages from the Bible. This activity may result in some discussion as to why a particular text is a favorite or why many people share the same favorites.

2. Develop a definition of stewardship as a group activity. Divide the group into pairs or triads and ask each small group to develop a list of five words or phrases that come to mind when they hear the word *stewardship*. Allow 3–5 minutes for this. Then bring the group back together and compile the lists by writing them on newsprint or a chalkboard.

3. Distribute copies of the worksheet and read through the definition of stewardship by John Westerhoff. Ask the following questions for reaction and discussion by the whole group:

- What do you think about this statement?
- What particular words or phrases are meaningful to you?
- Is there anything in this that is new for you?

Conclude by adding more words or phrases to the group definition of stewardship that might come out of the discussion of Westerhoff's statement.

4. With the broad, composite definition of stewardship in mind, ask the group to consider the Scripture passages listed and discuss the related questions on the worksheet. Again, form small groups. The same pairs or triads may want to work on all three texts, or the group may be divided into three groups to work, with each one assigned one of the three texts. Allow about 10–15 minutes for them to work and then bring the groups back together to share what they have discovered.

5. If there is time and you so choose, the questions listed on the worksheet may be applied to the favorite texts the group members offered in their introductions. Ask them to look or think back to what they said, or to another favorite Bible text, and see if there are stewardship lessons implied there.

6. Conclude with sharing ideas about how to encourage the biblical perspective of stewardship in the life of the church. If there is time, you may want to use other options given in the section on "Preparing the Session." Close with prayer.

THE PRICE OF FAITH

Bible-Based Stewardship

Definitions of Stewardship

ONE DEFINITION

Stewardship is what we do after we say we believe, that is, after we give our love, loyalty and trust to God, from whom each and every aspect of our lives comes as a gift. As members of God's household, we are subject to God's economy or stewardship, that is, God's plan to reconcile the whole world and bring creation to its proper end.

—John Westerhoff III,
Building God's People in a Materialistic Society

Applying the Stewardship Perspective

Questions to ask of the text:
1. What stewardship issues are raised?
2. What does it say about God and our relationship with God?
3. What is the stewardship lesson for us?

Psalm 104:24, 27–35

James 2:14–18

Matthew 6:19–21, 24–33

2. The Offering

> PURPOSE   The purpose of this study is to exam-
> ine and reflect on the beliefs implicit in the routine
> practice of receiving an offering as part of worship.
> The discussion is meant to encourage sharing
> among participants about their habits, assumptions,
> and intentions for giving in order to grow in faith
> and practices of stewardship.

Introduction

Although collecting alms and gifts for the poor has been prac-
ticed in the church since biblical times, the receiving of an
offering as part of Protestant liturgy was not common until
the mid-nineteenth century. Alms basins were sometimes
used in churches in medieval times to collect gifts brought
forward for the poor, and alms boxes were often attached to
a church wall or pillar to collect offerings from those who
came to worship. However, as part of the liturgy, the *offering*
itself in those times was the Eucharist. Later, during the
Reformation, there was an effort to separate the offering of
the Eucharist from the offering of gifts for the poor, and worshipers were reminded to give as they left the sanctuary.

When the Puritans and Separatists arrived in the New
World, the *Westminster Directory* of 1644 was still the guiding document, and the alms box at the rear of the sanctuary
made a clear connection between the sacred world of worship and the secular world and its needs. Voluntary giving of
alms after worship supported the poor, and support for the
minister and maintenance of the church was offered through
subscriptions and pew rents.

The nineteenth century saw the rapid development of
benevolent organizations and growing interest in mission on
the American frontier and in international lands. As part of this

change, collections, or offerings, became a regular part of worship. Although the first Presbyterian *Directory for Worship* was published in 1788, a chapter on the offering was not added until 1886. In that chapter, the instructions were to train every member to give systematically and to view such offerings as "a solemn act of worship." Denominational resources and books about church history may be researched for similar information about worship in churches other than Presbyterian.

Since that time, the offering of money has become an expected part of worship. Its place in the order of worship has been variously defined, but its meaning has always included an expression of gratitude to God and a response to the needs of the world.

Preparing the Session

Read through the entire session plan and the meditation. As you read the questions for discussion, think about your own responses and what those of your group might be. Adapt the questions or add to them to suit your group and your circumstances. When leading the discussion, encourage everyone to participate. Make copies of the meditation for every person in the group.

Optional Use for the Meditation and Prayer

Without the questions for discussion, the meditation and the prayer may be used effectively as a devotional for a meeting of the church governing board, the stewardship committee, or another group in the church.

In preparation, read through the text to become familiar with the phrasing and punctuation in order to allow listeners to follow and reflect. Preparing copies of the meditation and prayer for everyone is optional.

Leading the Session

1. Begin by introducing the subject of the study—share the information given in the Introduction. Speak briefly

about how the offering has become a routine part of worship and ask the participants for their thoughts. Note particular issues or questions that may be raised for later discussion.

2. Read the meditation aloud as participants listen or follow along.

3. Depending on the size of the group, you may want to divide them into smaller groups of two to four to encourage participation. Lead a discussion using the following questions:

- What words or phrases in this meditation are new for your understanding of the offering?
- Which words or phrases are particularly helpful?

4. As discussion leader, you may want to highlight or write on newsprint or chalkboard several phrases from the meditation to encourage responses from the group, such as these:

> *Touched by many hands. Passed on, passed by.*
> *And with our money we offer ourselves, our*
>   *values, our hopes and desires.*
> *The regular repeated call to discipleship and*
>   *ministry.*
> *A part of what already, always belongs to God.*

- How do you, or how does your family, make decisions about giving an offering?
- What is your experience of the offering in Sunday morning worship? How would you describe the mood? What are people doing?
- By what we do during the time of the offering, what is expressed of our beliefs about:

    our relationship with God
    what the church should be doing in the world
    our individual responsibilities for the world's
        needs

the offerings we see others give (children, older
  adults, well-to-do individuals, and others)
our sense of being a community of faith

- What is expressed of our beliefs by the way in which
  the offering is received? By what is said to introduce
  the offering and in our response of song or prayer?
- What do you think is being taught to the children by
  what they see happening at the time of the offering?
  What impressions are given to visitors and those who
  are new to the faith?
- Is there anything you would do differently? Is there
  anything you *will* do differently?

Closing

If the group has been divided for discussion, ask them to
come back together at this point. Bring closure to the session
by helping the group summarize the discussion. Conclude by
asking for responses to this question: *What new meaning or
insight will be on your mind during the offering next Sunday?*

If there is time, or if there are volunteers interested in getting together at another time, an offering prayer might be
written to use in worship. Another person might volunteer to
give a children's sermon using age-appropriate ideas and
information (these are always opportunities to teach the rest
of the congregation, too!).

The group may have other ideas of how to use what they
have learned.

The session may end with prayer.

Prayer

Holy God, Giver of every good and perfect gift, all that we
are and all that we have is from you. Help us to remember
from day to day that we are caretakers and stewards, not own-
ers, of our time, talents, and resources. Guide our efforts as
we earn, spend, save, and share what we have through the use
of your gifts to us. May we, as your people, be reflections of
your goodness and grace. We pray in Christ's name. Amen.

THE PRICE OF FAITH
The Offering
A Meditation

Offering plate, offering basket, offering box,
　Made of silver, brass, willow, plastic, or wood.
An empty place to be filled with our gifts.
　An opportunity, a challenge, an expression of grace.
Touched by many hands.
Passed on, passed by.
Passed back, brought forward.
　Offered and blessed.
Counted, accounted, and spent.

What was given? What was received?
　What was intended that our gifts would do
　For others? For the church? For ourselves?

Coins, dollar bills, handwritten checks,
　　noisy loose change or quietly sealed tight.
　Spontaneously given or a by careful decision, a private
　　choice made public.
Earned interest, cash dividends, paychecks—our income—
　Commissions, pensions, social security, welfare.

And with our money we offer ourselves, our values, our hopes
　and desires.
　Vocation, leisure, time—
　　out of a sense of duty, generosity, conviction,
　　　commitment?
With our money we offer ourselves,
　What we choose to be.
　What we could have bought. What we could have brought.

Offering plate, offering basket, offering box.
　The regular, repeated call to discipleship and ministry.
Giving, in gratitude to God,
　A part of what already, always belongs to God.

3. Where Your Treasure Is

A Bible Study about Priorities in Daily Living
Based on Matthew 6:19–24

> PURPOSE   This Bible study deals with the things we have and the priorities we choose in life. It is intended to encourage a thoughtful discussion of beliefs and practices concerning issues of consumption, the use of time and money, lifestyle, and the values and goals of individuals and the congregation.

Introduction

Particularly in Western culture, there is a prevalent desire to consume, accumulate, and store up things for ourselves. Our lifestyles give evidence of having more than basic necessities, and all that we have uses up time, energy, and resources to purchase, maintain, and protect. Economics, family status, personal ambitions, and pleasures, whether for good or not, influence the choices we make on a daily basis. Some of these choices are made consciously, others are by habit or default. The thoughts suggested in the meditation and the issues raised in the discussion questions are meant to facilitate conversation and probe difficult matters of faith that deal with priorities and goals in life.

Preparing the Session

Read through the entire session plan and the meditation. Find Bible commentaries that will give more background information about the text from Matthew. As you read the questions for discussion, think about your own responses and what those of your group might be. Adapt the questions or add to them to suit your group and your circumstances. When leading the discussion, encourage everyone to participate. Agreement and conclusions are not necessary. Make copies of the meditation for every person in the group.

Optional Use for the Meditation and Prayer

Without the questions for discussion, the meditation and the prayer may be used effectively as a devotional for a meeting of church leaders, the stewardship committee, or another group in the church.

In preparation, read through the text to become familiar with the phrasing and punctuation in order to allow listeners to follow and reflect. Preparing copies of the meditation and prayer for everyone is optional.

Leading the Session

1. After the group has gathered, briefly explain the subject of the Bible study. Read several of the discussion questions to prepare the participants for the kind of issues that will be raised.

2. Read, or have members of the group read, the Scripture passage from Matthew 6:19–24 and the meditation. After both readings, distribute copies of the meditation so everyone may refer to it during the discussion.

3. Lead a discussion using the following questions:

- How would you describe what you treasure—a place? a person? something you do? something you have?
- The Scripture text says that where our treasure is, there our hearts will be. Which is more helpful: To look first at where we spend our treasure (our time, money, and other resources)? Or to look first at where our hearts are (what we say we care about most)? What would we learn by looking at the record in our checkbook, for example?
- What are the resources—the people, organizations, the particular environment, time and abilities, for example—we have at our disposal? (Make a list of the group's responses.)

- What are the things we care about? (List the group's responses where they can be seen alongside the list of resources.)
- Discuss how our resources relate to the things we care about (for example, time as a resource and family as something we care about).
- To what extent do we allow choices about daily schedules and demands to happen by default?
- To what extent do we allow social, family, or cultural expectations to influence choices and priorities in lifestyle and spending habits, and where do we find pleasure and satisfaction?
- Consider all that you treasure. Is it enough? Is there enough to share?

4. Another line of discussion could follow these questions about the life of the congregation:

- What does our church budget show about our treasures and priorities as a congregation?
- What would we want to be different? How would we go about making that difference?

Closing

To end the discussion and study, help the group summarize what has been said. Conclude with prayers offered by participants thanking God for the treasures of life, or close with the prayer that follows the meditation.

Prayer

Loving God, we look to you to guide us in all we say and do. Fill our hearts and minds with your wisdom and will. Make us your people. Direct our ways as we seek the treasures of your love and peace. May we know your presence within and among us. We pray through Christ. Amen.

THE PRICE OF FAITH

Where Your Treasure Is

A Meditation

Where your treasure is, there is your heart also.
    It is a statement of fact that begs questions of faith:
    Where *is* your treasure? Where is your *heart*?
The place is already known.
    It is, by choice or by default, given to some endeavor,
        some desire,
        some hope for fulfillment and purpose.
There is a human, spiritual need to find
    a place where we can feel secure and confident,
    a place where we belong.
For we will believe in something or someone to give
     meaning to life.

Credo, "I believe."
    It means "I set my heart."
Surrounded by change,
    distracted by many colorful, transient possibilities
        for pleasure and meaning,
    we seek somewhere to set our hearts.

We seek a worthy treasure,
    a place for our homelessness of mind
    and our restlessness of spirit.
A place where the door is always open to us,
    to those we love,
    and to strangers.
Where there is room for all to gather at the table
    and enough for all to eat.
A safe and comfortable place where we can express
    our greatest joy
    and expose our deepest doubt.

A place to keep what we treasure,
    a place that is our treasure,
    a place to set our hearts.

4. An Autobiography about Money

A PERSONAL HISTORY OF PRACTICES AND ATTITUDES

> PURPOSE   This session is intended to raise our awareness of the people and experiences that have affected our practices, habits, and attitudes about money and to reflect on the continuing significance these have as we deal particularly with issues of giving to people, causes, and the church.

Introduction

Money is a powerful part of our individual lives and our common culture. The importance of money can be in opposition to Christian faith when we allow it to define value and worth for what is good in life. Yet money is also a vital tool with which we can carry out the ministry and mission of the church. Money is an effective means of exchange when it is given or shared in order to feed, clothe, and give shelter, compensate for work accomplished, or provide opportunities for bringing our personal or corporate visions to reality. Earning, spending, investing, saving, and giving money, when it is part of a generous, selfless lifestyle, is an expression of grace and gratitude for the world God has created.

This exercise is intended to help individuals grow in their understanding of the meaning of money in their lives and how their attitudes, habits, and practices in using money have developed. Memories from childhood and teenage years and stories of significant persons and events continue to influence and determine our attitudes about money and what we do with it. Our faith is inextricably bound to these experiences and to what we believe is our calling to be stewards of God's gifts.

Preparing the Session

This exercise is meant to be shared among a group of people concerned with and interested in the disciplines of stewardship. It is not a written exercise; it is storytelling between and among participants with one person's thoughts provoking the memories and insights of others. The depth to which anyone chooses to share memories or feelings about those memories is each individual's choice, and this should be made clear by the leader.

Plan to spend about one hour for the whole exercise, regardless of the size of the group. The sharing of stories will take at least 45 minutes; the summary discussion may last 10 to 20 minutes or more, depending on the size of the group and on how the leader chooses to bring closure (see options for closing).

Do not make copies of the questions for the participants, since the exercise depends on the progression of memories and ideas. Having all of the questions seen at once would distract from the storytelling and listening.

Leading the Session

1. Introduce the exercise by explaining briefly what will be done, the amount of time to expect in sharing stories and in discussion, and the purpose for such an exercise. Refer to the information given in the sections above.

2. Divide the group into pairs (allow three in a group if it is not possible to divide evenly). Provide paper and pens or pencils. Since the participants will not have the questions in front of them, they may want to jot down a few notes as they get involved in their sharing.

3. Read the first set of questions about childhood memories and allow 8–10 minutes for sharing stories. You will have to interrupt the conversations each time to move on to the next set of questions. Explain that they can pick up where they left off and then move on to answer the questions you have just read.

4. Read the second set of questions about money in teenage years and allow another 8–10 minutes. Do the same for the remaining two sets of questions. You may want to remind participants that they have permission *not* to share some of their experiences or feelings if they so choose.

5. After the final conversations about the last set of questions, gather the group back together and use the following questions for discussion.

- What do you think you were taught as you were growing up about getting, having, using, and giving money?
- How are these lessons and experiences still influencing your attitudes and habits about money?
- If you could identify a particular person or event as significant and influential in your experience of dealing with money, who or what would that be and what lesson did you learn?
- How are your habits of giving to the church the same or different from other opportunities to give?

Closing

As the discussion ends, help the group summarize what was said and learned. One of the three following options may be used to conclude the session:

- Scripture reading and prayer (4–5 minutes)
    Suggestions: Psalm 24:1–6; Matthew 6:19–21;
    Luke 12:13–21; 2 Corinthians 8:8–15;
    2 Corinthians 9:6–15.
- Bible study and prayer (20–30 minutes)
    Use one of the Scripture readings suggested above for a study and discussion with help from Bible commentaries.
- Prayer (1–2 minutes)

THE PRICE OF FAITH

An Autobiography about Money

Three Sets of Questions for Discussion

Childhood

When you were a child, was your family rich or poor? When were you aware of the differences?

Did you ever receive money as a gift? From whom? What did you do with it?

Did you receive an allowance? Did you have to earn it? What did you do with the money?

Teenage Years

When you were a teenager, did family money (your own family's and others') have anything to do with friendships, extracurricular activities, or vocational expectations?

Did you have a job outside the home? What happened to that money?

The Present Time

How does your family handle significant purchases?

Do you sometimes go shopping to make yourself feel better?

Do you usually compare what you have with those who have more or those who have less than you do?

To what extent do you equate your value as a person with what you earn or with what you own?

What are your giving habits to
solicitors on the phone?
civic groups, schools, colleges, and universities?
the arts, public radio, and television?
the church—pledging? special offerings?

5. Faith and Money

A BIBLE STUDY ABOUT WORK, EARNINGS, AND STEWARDSHIP
BASED ON JAMES 2:14–18

> PURPOSE The purpose of this study is to examine the connections between what we do and say and what we believe. By hearing the Scripture text from the New Testament book of James read in new ways, we may discover a fuller understanding of the meaning and practice of faithful Christian stewardship.

Introduction

The tension between faith and works as evidence of what one truly believes has been a matter for debate and discussion since the time of the early Christian church. The text from James raises the issue clearly.

When discussion of these verses moves to the context of stewardship, the idea of *works* may be understood beyond good deeds and works of mission. In this sense, stewardship includes all we do to live faithfully: the work we do to earn a living, how we spend our time and money, and how we give it away and perform other acts of hospitality.

A rereading of the text from James may bring new awareness of the interrelatedness of belief and action. This study encourages us to reflect on what we say and do to share with others the meaning and concrete expressions of faith.

Preparing the Session

Read through the entire session plan and become familiar with the Scripture lesson from James and the paraphrased version printed on the worksheet. You may want background information for the text—the historical context of James, the theories of authorship, and its general content. Bible dictionaries and commentaries will be helpful. Other perspectives may also be found in reading a variety of Bible translations and versions.

Become familiar with the worksheet and questions for discussion. Consider your own responses and think through what responses might come from the group.

Leading the Session

1. Begin by introducing the subject of the session, which is faith, and how it relates to and is expressed by what we do. A brief overview of the book of James may be helpful to share with the group. Further explain that each of us brings our own perspective, shaped by experience, to reading and understanding of the Bible. This study looks at the Scripture text from a perspective of stewardship.

2. After introductory comments, ask one of the participants to read James 2:14–18. If different versions and translations of the Bible are available, have more than one read to the group. Then read the paraphrased version given in this session.

3. After reading the paraphrased version, hand out copies of the worksheet so participants can read the text and move on to a discussion of it. Use the following questions to guide the conversation, which may take place with the group as a whole or with the group divided into pairs or triads.

- What issues are raised when our *works* are translated into *the earnings from our work?*
- How is our vocational work evidence of the works of our faith?
- What issues are raised when we think of our works of faith as everything we do in life?
- How does stewardship take on meaning in this text?

4. With the group as a whole, or still working in smaller groups, ask the participants to expand the discussion of stewardship by filling in the blanks at the bottom of the worksheet with words and phrases such as vocation, time, and home.

Closing

Bring the group together and help them summarize the discussion. Ask them which substituted words for *works* fit the discussion and their experience, and which did not. Ask them what difference this study has made or will make for them. Encourage them to read the Bible from a perspective of stewardship—the care and responsible use of all of our resources and gifts from God. End with a prayer of thanksgiving and commitment.

THE PRICE OF FAITH
Faith and Money
A Bible Study Based on James 2:14–18

A Paraphrased Version of the Text

What good is it, my brothers and sisters, if you say you have faith but it has nothing to do with *money?* Can faith save you? If a brother or sister is naked and lacks daily food, and one of you says to them, "Go in peace; keep warm and eat your fill," and yet you do not supply their bodily needs, what is the good of that? So faith by itself, if it has nothing to do with *money*, is dead.

But someone will say, "You have faith and I have *my concerns about money*." Show me your faith apart from *the way you handle your money*, and I by *the way I handle my money* will show you my faith. (Author's paraphrase)

Questions for Discussion

1. What issues are raised when our "works" are translated into the "earnings from our work?"
2. How is our vocational work evidence of the works of our faith?
3. How does stewardship take on meaning in this text?

Fill in the Blanks

- Use other words and phrases such as vocation, time, and home.
- What other words or phrases could be used that have to do with our stewardship of God's gifts?

What good is it, my brothers and sisters, if you say you have faith but it has nothing to do with _____? Can faith save you? If a brother or sister is naked and lacks daily food, and one of you says to them, "Go in peace; keep warm and eat your fill," and yet you do not supply their bodily needs, what is the good of that? So faith by itself, if it has nothing to do with _____, is dead.

But someone will say, "You have faith and I have *concerns about* _____." Show me your faith apart from your _____, and I by my _____ will show you my faith.

6. Spare Change

AN EXERCISE IN ASKING AND GIVING

PURPOSE The purpose of this exercise has many
dimensions. As an introductory activity, it helps
participants begin to consider the subject of stewardship in a concrete and personal way, and it serves
to acquaint the participants with one another. At
another level, the exercise raises issues of personal
and societal attitudes about the value of money, how
needs can be met by giving money, and the ways in
which wealth is distributed. At yet another level, the
exercise points to theological beliefs that are
reflected in our behavior and our beliefs about community, responsibility, charity, and stewardship.

Introduction

Financial stewardship concerns our beliefs and attitudes about
money. Many people are uncomfortable asking for money,
even for the church or other good causes. Sometimes we are
uncomfortable being asked to give. This activity requires both
asking and being asked, but does so without the seriousness of
a planned, personal call for a donation. Nevertheless, it is a *real*
experience with money exchanging hands.

Preparing the Session

As you prepare to lead the session, become familiar with the
activity and read through the questions for discussion. Think
through your own responses to both the exercise and the
questions. When leading the session, keep track of the time
as the asking and giving are going on to allow adequate time
for the follow-up discussion. Refrain from making any judg-
ment of behavior, and encourage only those comments that
help the group raise awareness among themselves of the varied motives and reasons for giving or not giving when asked
for a contribution. Facilitate a comparison of the feelings and

reactions of asking and being asked. Allow the discussion to remain open-ended as you lead into the closing.

Leading the Session

1. Ask participants to take out the coins they have in their purse or pocket. Explain that they should be prepared to give and receive that money from one another based on the needs they perceive and their ability to give. Make clear that they will not be keeping the money regardless of whether they give away all they have or whether they receive everything the other group members have to give.

2. Explain that each of them is to think of a need to which they and the others could give—it should be a real need that is personal or global, community-based, or having to do with an individual they know. Each participant is to convince the others to contribute to the need he or she supports.

3. Allow time for everyone to think of a particular cause they would support and of what they will say to the others as they try to convince them to give. Then take 10–15 minutes, depending on the size of the group, to interact and have money change hands. This part ends when the group has reached a conclusion—some persons may have kept their own money to give to the cause they support, all money may have been given to just one person whose cause everyone ended up supporting, or the money may have been distributed among several causes. Individuals also may have divided their money and given to more than one cause. Whatever the conclusion, the money remains on the table.

4. Bring the group together for discussion using the following questions:

- What did the participants contribute? A lot or a little? What were the feelings about the amount they had available to give?

- Was it all they had in their pockets or purses?
- Was some held back, and if so, for what reason?
- As the class members dealt with one another, what convinced any one of them to give their money to some cause other than their own?
- How was the decision made about how much to give?
- How was the decision made about how much to ask for?
- What theological beliefs are evident in the ways causes or needs are represented?
- What theological beliefs are evident in the decisions to ask for or give money?
- How does this activity compare with other experiences of benevolent giving—

  Salvation Army buckets at Christmas?
  Cancer Society at the door of your home?
  United Way annual campaign?
  The congregation's annual financial pledge campaign?
  The Sunday morning offering plate?

5. Conclude this part of the activity by explaining that the money they have given and collected will, in fact, be contributed to a good cause. Depending on how the asking and giving exercise ended, the moneys should go to the causes as designated. If several causes were chosen and the money amounts are relatively small, the group may want to choose just one cause to receive the whole amount. Individuals in the group, or you as the leader, may take the responsibility for seeing that the donations are made.

Closing

A prayer of dedication for the money being given and for all the needs represented would be an appropriate way to end the session.

If more time is available, a Scripture reading with discussion would be an alternative. A suggested reading from the New Testament is 1 Corinthians 9:6–15, which includes the statement that "God loves a cheerful giver." Read the text and lead a brief discussion of what it would mean to be "cheerful" in our giving. Additional background information for the leader may be found in Bible commentaries.

7. Charity Begins at Home

A CASE STUDY ABOUT ATTITUDES AND RELATIONSHIPS
BETWEEN GIVERS AND RECIPIENTS

> PURPOSE   This case study examines the dynam-
> ics of changing attitudes and relationships within
> the community of the church when the recipients of
> mission giving become active members of the con-
> gregation. The study enables a discussion of
> motives, beliefs, and expectations of individual
> members and the congregation as a whole.

Introduction

When church people give money, food, and clothing for the
poor, they generally expect their gifts to go to people and
places they will not see, whether it is to a foreign land or a
different part of town from where they live and work. What
we say and feel about giving may well take on a different
meaning when we can see what is done with the gifts we give.
Different values and different ideas about lifestyle challenge
our generosity and the expectations we have of those who
receive our gifts.

Preparing the Session

Read through the entire session, the case study, and the questions for discussion. Consider your own responses and what
other issues might arise from the discussion. You may have
to choose between using the first set of discussion questions
in part 3 of "Leading the Lesson" or the questions in part 4,
due to time. If you choose to focus on the questions in part 4,
be sure to at least list the characters and describe the sequence
of events in the case study. Make enough copies of the case
study itself for each person in the group. Be prepared to open
and/or close the session with prayer.

Leading the Session

1. After offering a prayer, if you choose to do so, begin by introducing the nature of case studies as incidents from actual experience that raise issues that are typical and generally affect us all. Briefly describe the subject matter of this case using the information given in the Introduction above.

2. Distribute copies of the case study and give the group enough time to read it. Instruct them to make note of the people and the issues involved for the discussion to follow.

3. Lead the group through an analysis of the case study.

- List the main characters by name or role.
- Describe the sequence of events to make sure everyone understands what happened.
- Ask for general reactions and responses.
- If the discussion does not bring out any mention of how they might have reacted if they were involved, ask the following questions: What would you have done if you were the elders Bob and Matt? Minister Mary Lou? The one who had given the girls new outfits? Can you imagine yourself as one of the Watsons?

4. Depending on the size of your group, you may want to continue working with everyone together or you may want to divide them into smaller groups of three to five. Use all or only some of these next questions according to the time available and the direction of the group's interest.

- As members of the church, what can we consider private? What are appropriate concerns of the faith community about its own members?
- What are the responsibilities we have as church members for sharing what we have? What are our

understandings of a fair distribution of wealth? How is this done by individual members? How is this done by the congregation through its benevolent giving?

- What are the responsibilities we have as church members for caring for the needs of one another? Spiritual needs? Educational needs? Financial needs?
- What happens when the poor expect to receive, or when they are not especially grateful?
- In what ways do we expect and even require people who come to our church to be like us? Are there limits to acceptable diversity? Are there basic requirements of attire, attitude, and behavior?

Closing

Close the session by asking the members of the group to respond to the discussion of the case study in terms of their faith. Read each of the following statements one at a time and ask how each relates to the circumstances and individuals of the case and to their own beliefs:

- *Humanity is created in the image of God.*
- *The Church is the body of Christ made up of many parts.*
- *We are called to be followers of Christ.*
- *God loves a cheerful giver.*

If there is time, you may want to ask the group to write a brief stewardship statement of faith that could be used in worship, printed in the church newsletter, or used for the year's annual financial stewardship campaign.

End with a prayer offered by the leader or one of the participants and include the thoughts and concerns raised during the session.

THE PRICE OF FAITH
Charity Begins at Home
Case Study

Covenant Church is located in a small Midwestern town with a population of approximately 14,000. The church has a long history that parallels the changes and development of the town, and some of the community's most influential citizens were members of the church. For more than 175 years, the church and the town have held a certain prominence in their part of the state. At the turn of the century, the town was a thriving center of manufacturing and shipping. Shifts in industry and transportation created an economic decline that had one long-term benefit: the preservation of historic homes and public buildings. Recently the town once more has begun to revive its economy by successfully developing its potential for tourism and by attracting business, so that small manufacturing plants have been built in the area.

Covenant Church has always been located downtown in the heart of the historic district, and its membership has always included some of the well-established families, the town leaders, and the decision-makers. Presently, the membership is about 300, and it consists of long-standing members, newcomers to the community, old and young, of mostly middle and upper-middle income levels. A growing number of young families with children has stimulated the growth of the church program and the church's sense of well-being and promise.

After close to twenty-five years of declining church membership, attendance, and activity, the congregation is feeling the joys and the challenges of having new faces, new ideas, and new directions for ministry and mission.

Into the life of this congregation has come a family who has recently moved to town—the Watsons, a family of four. For Jim, the father, it was coming back to his hometown. For Linda, the mother, who had grown up in a large city, and to their two little girls, Naomi and Belinda, it was a new experience. The family, as did the father's family, depends on welfare. Both parents in this young family have physical limitations in their sight and receive disability payments. By their appearance and behavior, they are noticeably different from everyone else in the congregation on a Sunday morning.

At first, and especially after they had come for several Sundays, they were well received by the church. They were encouraged to come to coffee hour after worship, Naomi and Belinda were invited to join the children's choir, and the whole family was included in church activities. They lived eight blocks from the church and usually walked, but when the weather was bad, people in the congregation took turns driving them to and from worship and other meetings and events.

It was obvious that the parents and the children did not have as much as others and needed some things. When winter came, the most obvious need was for warm coats and boots. People approached them cautiously, not wanting to offend them in any way. They offered to share what they had outgrown or to purchase new things. A few people asked them directly, others made offers through the minister or the deacons. When the Christmas season came, one member, a grandmother with two young grandchildren of her own in the congregation, anonymously gave complete new holiday outfits to the two girls—dresses, shoes and socks, and all. Books and toys were given by others. And one of the deacons' food baskets was delivered to their door.

It was not long before Linda and Jim joined the church. The whole family attended regularly. Belinda and Naomi were in church school and choir. Linda joined the adult choir, volunteered to teach, and became active on the worship committee. Jim helped with maintenance, setting up tables and chairs for dinners and meetings. He became a regular in the kitchen on Sunday mornings as coffee and cookies were prepared for Fellowship Hour.

No one asked, of course, about their financial status or how they were getting along on food stamps and welfare checks. But in a small town, people know such things from living and working with one another or can find out easily if they are curious. Both Linda and Jim found part-time work such as neighborhood newspaper routes and odd jobs. On the whole, they have been admired for their industriousness. Especially impressive to some is the dollar bill Jim puts in the offering plate each Sunday morning.

A small town does not allow first impressions to last very long. As time has gone by, more of the members of the church have encountered this family in various ways outside of church. Through the school where some members are teachers, the Watsons are known for continually asking for financial help. Church member Sarah Mane has Naomi in her fourth-grade class. Local agencies repeatedly receive requests from the parents for help with utility and rent bills. Jim and Linda regularly overdraw their account at the bank.

Though both parents are legally blind, they bought a used car. They adopted a dog and several cats. The Watson's front yard is one continuous yard sale, and people going by have seen the clothing and toys they shared with them for sale, even the new holiday outfits.

Jim and Linda also approach the church for help—asking for food from the pantry and then money for catching up with overdue telephone and heating bills. Although the usual limit for financial help has been $25, close to $100 was given so they could avoid having the heat turned off and to have their telephone reconnected. Bill Stout, a member who happens to work for the telephone company, learned that the reconnection included call waiting and other extras.

Through a literacy program at the library, Bob Black, another church member, volunteered to teach Jim how to read. And as the requests for financial help have continued to come to the church, Bob Black, who is a retired business executive, and Matt Langdon, a lawyer with financial expertise, joined Mary Lou Munford, the minister, in helping the parents learn something about budgeting and financial planning. It was a somewhat conditional arrangement; further financial help from the church entailed a commitment from Linda and Jim to look seriously at their financial situation and determine ways in which to survive for the present and plan for the future.

Bob, Matt, and Mary Lou did not consider the effort successful. Jim and Linda had listened politely and readily divulged all financial information. At the conclusion of three sessions together, the church folks who wanted to help felt overwhelmed by the debt the family had incurred and discouraged by the lack of prospects for change. The couple seemed unbothered by the circumstances and unwilling to change.

Seldom are such congregations representative of much diversity in economic status. The arrival of this family into the life of the church seemed at first to be an opportunity for everyone to learn and grow from the experience. A few members, including Sally and Martha who are on the board of deacons, were skeptical and cynical from the start. They suspected that the Watsons had come only with the intention of asking for and expecting financial help.

What is the church to do? What is Mary Lou's responsibility? They have come again, this time asking for help in meeting the payments for their home, a rent-to-buy arrangement, and they are three months behind.

8. The Mission Front

A CASE STUDY ABOUT BUDGET DECISIONS
OF A CHURCH SESSION

> PURPOSE   This case study examines the dynam-
> ics of financial decision-making among congre-
> gational leaders. It raises questions about who
> initiates ideas that have an impact on the budget, the
> authority of the congregational governing board,
> the role of the pastor, and attitudes about local needs
> and worldwide mission.

Introduction

Money and missions generally go together in church discussions of budgets and financial planning. Even though the
greater proportion of any congregation's annual budget is
used for supporting the program and staff of the local church,
the intent in allocating funds is to give away a percentage to
mission. Debate often occurs, however, over whether those
mission funds should be spent locally to support a community food pantry, youth shelter, or other service organiza-
tion, sent to international missions of the congregation's
own choosing, or sent to denominational offices to support
national and worldwide mission.

The farther away the locus of mission, the more difficult, it
seems, to have the interest and enthusiasm of the church. In
this case study, the distance was not only in location but also
in time. The particular mission being presented had its roots in
past generations of the congregation, and much of its significance was forgotten or meaningless to the current members.

This study may be particularly useful in situations where
there is interest in celebrating church history, where there is
debate about the appropriate use of funds or discussion
among the leadership of the church about how to introduce
new ideas and programs.

Preparing the Session

Read through the entire session, the case study, and the questions for discussion. Consider your own responses and what other issues might arise from the discussion. Make enough copies of the case study itself for each person in the group. Be prepared to open and/or close the session with prayer.

Leading the Session

1. After offering a prayer, if you choose to do so, begin by introducing the nature of case studies as incidents from actual experience that raise issues that are typical and generally affect us all. Briefly describe the subject matter of this case using the information given in the Introduction above.

2. Distribute copies of the case study and give the group enough time to read it. Instruct them to make note of the people and the issues involved, for the discussion to follow.

3. Lead the group through an analysis of the case study.

- List the main characters by name or role.
- Describe the sequence of events.

4. Depending on the size of your group, you may want to continue working with everyone together or you may want to divide them into smaller groups of three to five. Use all or only some of these next questions according to the time available and the direction of the group's interest.

- At what points could the pastor and elders have stopped for discussion in order to avoid the conflict? What needed to be discussed?
- How could the idea have been presented so that there might have been interest and enthusiasm from the whole governing board?
- What are the alternatives now for Rhoda Bennet, the pastor?

- What are the implications for the future in terms of relationships and how the leadership of the church functions, particularly where money is involved?
- What needs to happen? Why?
- What are the beliefs and issues of faith at stake?

5. After discussing the questions regarding the case, lead the group through the following questions that deal with the connections and implications for your own congregational life. If the group has been divided for discussion, you may want to bring them back together for this part.

- Is there any specific mission that has a history in our congregation? Is it still familiar to most members and supported in any way? Is it something to highlight in church communications and the budget, or is it no longer existing or relevant?
- What would it take to revive a program or event that no longer goes on in the church? What would it take to start a new one? Who should be involved? What are the financial implications? What barriers would there be?
- How are decisions about money and budgeting made in our congregation? How are disagreements handled? Are there clear priorities? Is there a generally agreed upon understanding of the place of mission in the life of the church?

Closing

Close the discussion by asking the members of the group to complete this statement: *One thing I learned about money-related decisions in the church is* . . .

End with a prayer offered by the leader or one of the participants, and include the thoughts and concerns raised during the session. As an alternative, a prayer or litany may be written in advance or copied from a resource to be read in unison by the whole group.

THE PRICE OF FAITH
The Mission Front
Case Study

In 1890, Albert Raney, the son of an established and beloved family of the Presbyterian Church in Livingston, a small Midwestern town, responded to the call to be a missionary in Korea. The Raneys had been among the first settlers of the town in pioneer days. They and their descendants were known for their success in business, their leadership in the church, and their contributions to the life of the community. Albert's missionary efforts eventually resulted in the founding of medical missions, hospitals, and schools, along with spreading the Christian gospel in Korea. His children and their families carried on the missionary tradition for several generations. However, over time, the family ties to Livingston disappeared. Some members of the family died and were buried there. Others moved away. Finally, there were few people in town or in the Livingston Presbyterian Church who remembered anything of the Raney missionary family and their roots.

In contrast, Korean Presbyterians kept the memories alive, even those who immigrated and settled in the United States. One of the Korean Presbyterian churches is located within a hundred miles of Livingston. Upon learning of their proximity to the place where Korean Presbyterianism had its roots, Samuel Chin, the pastor, and leaders of the Korean congregation wanted to plan a visit.

Letters and telephone conversations between Rhoda Bennet, pastor of Livingston Presbyterian Church, and Samuel Chin confirmed arrangements, and the trip was scheduled; the Korean church would come to visit the home congregation of the family that had meant so much to them and their Presbyterian heritage. A caravan of cars brought about forty members of the Korean congregation—the choir, several elders, and the pastor—for a Sunday evening program and dinner. There were about the same number from the Livingston church (which has a membership of three hundred).

The evening was a wonderful success. The Korean Presbyterians were in awe of the place where the missionary family had once worshiped and prayed. The members of the Livingston church who attended became interested and appreciative of a part of their history they had not known. And members of both congregations enjoyed the time of worship and fellowship together. Many people said afterward, "We should do this again."

About three years later, the congregation of Livingston Presbyterian Church celebrated its bicentennial anniversary. The occasion was a good reason to do some much-needed maintenance and renovation on the facilities. A fund-raising campaign was launched, but there was concern among members of the session (the governing board of the congregation) that money given should not be limited to the needs of the congregation, but should also include new mission efforts. A decision was made to set aside 10 percent of whatever money was raised to be used for some yet-to-be-determined mission cause or causes.

It was not until after the renovation was complete and the celebration was over that serious discussion began about how to use the 10 percent that had been set aside, which amounted to $10,000. In the meantime, there had been turnover on the session and some of the elders who had been enthusiastic about mission were no longer there with voice and vote. Discussion went on over a period of months and decisions were made a little at a time. Some of the money was to stay in the community and was divided between two agencies serving children and youth. About half of the original amount was sent to the denomination as Livingston Presbyterian Church's share of a special fund for mission.

More than six months later, a portion still remained, a little less than $2,000, without any decision made for its use. About that time, Rhoda received a letter from Martin Raney, a missionary who had been in Korea and a descendant of

Albert Raney. He was retiring from his work and planning a trip across the country to visit family and friends and hoped to stop by Livingston and the church along the way.

Rhoda took the letter to the next Session meeting and suggested that this might be an opportunity to focus on mission—to invite the Korean church back for another visit, raise awareness among members of that particular mission and celebrate their historical connection to a part of the world where the Presbyterian church is experiencing phenomenal growth. Rhoda suggested that some of the remaining, undesignated mission money might be used to help Martin and his family with expenses for travel and lodging so they could be part of a weekend program.

By common consent, the Session approved looking into the possibilities, and Rhoda began corresponding with Martin Raney, offering suggestions for travel and lodging along with ideas for a mission event in which he would participate. Martin responded enthusiastically, and before long, actual dates were scheduled and plans were made. The session was kept informed all along, and several elders were willing to take some responsibility in helping to plan the whole event. However, it was only when the final costs of airline tickets were presented that it became clear that not everyone approved of the effort.

At the session meeting that was held only six weeks before the mission weekend, which included a dinner, an evening program, and Martin Raney as a guest preacher Sunday morning, the discontent surfaced. It had been assumed by some of the elders and the pastor that the undesignated mission money would be used to pay for any expenses of the event, mainly the travel and lodging for two. Tom Rich and Agnes Miller had apparently been against the whole idea from the start and pointed out that no formal decision had ever been made to use those funds in this way. The discussion went in numerous directions about how mission money should be spent, how local needs of the poor were far more important than having a program, how Martin Raney must be taking advantage of the Livingston church to pay for his personal travel to family and friends, and how there really wasn't much interest among church members to attend the upcoming event.

Finally, Agnes made a motion to withdraw the invitation to the Raneys and cancel the plans. Hoping to salvage something, Nancy Conner proposed amending the motion so as to withdraw financial support; the event could go on, but the money would not be spent on it. Rhoda pointed out that the invitation had already been made and how awkward it would be to withdraw, especially so close to the planned date. Nevertheless, the amendment passed, and then Tom and Agnes pushed to have a vote taken. It was clear that the usual process of consensus would not work, and the call was for a show of hands. The motion passed by a narrow margin.

Suddenly, what some elders saw as a significant event in the life of the church that was meant to be positive and exciting had become devastatingly negative. Rhoda was left to communicate the changes to Martin Raney and his wife and to the Korean congregation, as well as to the congregation of the Livingston Presbyterian Church.

9. The Sunday Morning Offering

A HISTORY AND STUDY OF THE PLACE OF THE OFFERING IN WORSHIP

> PURPOSE   The purpose of this session is to examine the ways in which the offering is received as part of Sunday morning worship. By looking at what the practices have been in the past and what they are in the present, participants will explore the theological meanings and implications of the different ways.

Introduction

It is not unusual that there are aspects of worship in which we participate without knowing or questioning why. The time of the offering may be one of them.

Although collecting alms and gifts for the poor has been known in the church since biblical times, the receiving of an offering as part of Protestant liturgy was not common until the mid-nineteenth century. Alms basins were sometimes used in medieval times to collect gifts brought forward for the poor, and alms boxes were often attached to a church wall or pillar to collect offerings from those who came to worship. However, as part of the liturgy, the *offering* itself in those times was the Eucharist. Later, during the Reformation, there was an effort to separate the offering of the Eucharist from the offering of gifts for the poor, and worshipers were reminded to give as they left the sanctuary.

When the Puritans and Separatists arrived in the New World, the *Westminster Directory* of 1644 was still the guiding document, and the alms box at the rear of the sanctuary made a clear connection between the sacred world of worship and the secular world and its needs. Voluntary giving of alms after worship supported the poor, and support for the minister and maintenance of the church was collected through subscriptions and pew rents.

The nineteenth century saw the rapid development of benevolent organizations and growing interest in mission on the American frontier and throughout the world. As part of this change, collections, or offerings, became a regular part of worship. Although the first Presbyterian *Directory for Worship* was published in 1788, a chapter on the offering was not added until 1886. In that chapter, the instructions were to train every member to give systematically and to view such offerings as "a solemn act of worship." Denominational resources and books about church history may be consulted for similar information about worship in churches other than Presbyterian.

Since that time, the offering of money has become an expected part of worship. Its place in the order of worship has been variously defined, but its meaning has always included the expression of gratitude to God and a response to the needs of the world.

This session is intended to lead participants through a study of Presbyterian service books as an example of the changes in practices of receiving the offering and what these changes say about what we believe concerning the offering.

Preparing the Session

Read through the entire session, including the Introduction and the following sets of questions. Become familiar with the information in order to present it briefly to the group. Make copies of the worksheet for everyone.

Leading the Session

1. Begin by giving a brief introduction to what the session is about—the offering and its place in worship. Explain that we will be learning something of the history of the offering and looking at our own experiences and beliefs.

2. To start everyone thinking about what is done in worship when receiving the offering, ask the participants to write

down the order they are most accustomed to in their experience. Ask them to include the following information:

- What is the place of the offering in the order of worship?
- Who takes up the offering?
- Is there a sung response (Doxology or other)?
- Is a prayer offered? If so, what type of prayer, who offers it, and is it spoken before or after the offerings are collected?
- Who are the people involved at each point in the offering?
- What is your own usual part in the liturgy of the offering?

3. After everyone has written their responses, take time to compare experiences. Depending on the size of the group, you may want to divide them into smaller groups to encourage conversation.

- Did you have any trouble remembering what is done?
- Are your experiences different in any way from the others'?
- Have you had many different experiences in the past?
- What do you know of other traditions?

4. Before going on, give a brief overview of the history of the offering in worship, using the information given in the Introduction. Lead into the worksheet showing all the Presbyterian service books, if they are available, or listing them, their dates, and relevant information for the offering.

5. Share with the group the understanding that what we *do* conveys what we *believe*—and that this understanding underlies our search when examining the changes regarding the offering in the service books, and in our own experience of the offering in worship.

6. Hand out the worksheet. Read through the instructions with the group and answer any questions about what is to be done. Allow time for individuals or small groups to use the worksheet to prepare for the next discussion.

7. Lead a discussion with the whole group using what has been learned from the service books. Be sure to include all elements of the offering listed in the left column of the chart even if some of those elements have not been selected by the participants.

Include points such as the following:

- Implications of where the offering is placed—before the sermon, after, earlier in the service.
- The type of prayer offered and what it says about our beliefs about the ways in which God acts in our world and our response.
- How we can interpret the blanks on the chart, the places where guidelines are not given.

8. Return to the outlines the participants wrote of their own experiences of the offering in worship. Ask them to make comparisons with what is described on the worksheet. What are the theological implications of what they do now—who gets to participate by giving an offering (everyone, including the minister and the choir)? What does the way in which the offering is received say about our relationship with God? What do we expect God to do with our offerings—and what parts do we continue to play after money is given? What aspect of the time of the offering is most meaningful? Is there any part they would change? Why?

Closing

Help the group to summarize what has been discussed. Conclude the session by asking participants to share with the group their response to the following unfinished sentence: *During the offering time in worship next Sunday, I will* . . .

A prayer may be offered to end the time together.

THE PRICE OF FAITH

The Sunday Offering

The Offering in Presbyterian Service Books

*Aspects of the Worship Service Related to the Offering
from the Five Service Books according to the Date of Publication*

	1906	1932
Announcements in worship	offering immediately after	"announcements and offering"
Place in order of worship	after General Prayer, before sermon	after General Prayer, before sermon
Communion Table	offering brought to Table	"brought forward and presented"
Minister's role	calls for and prays	calls for and prays
Who gathers the offering	church officers	church officers
"Act of worship"	[stated in 1886 *Directory for Worship*]	first time stated in service book
Doxology	———	doxology or hymn of praise
Prayer	for God's blessing	dedication
Communion	———	———

1. Choose two of the boxes in the far left column and compare the changes in all five service books regarding this aspect of the offering.

2. Consider what is being demonstrated and taught by what is done, when it is done in the worship service, and who is doing it

3. What do our actions convey about
   our worship of God
   our understanding of what we own and what we have to offer to God
   our relationships within the worshiping community of faith.

4. List three actions or statements for group discussion.

Offering (cont.)

Aspects (cont.)

1946	1970	1993
offering immediately after	announcements before Prayers of People	[no mention of announcements]
General Prayer, then "here or after sermon"	after sermon before Invitation	after sermon, first part of Eucharist
———	———	brought forward; minister or elders prepare Table
calls for with scripture and prays	calls for and prays	———
———	———	———
———	———	———
doxology or other response	doxology or other response	doxology, hymn or spiritual
dedication	thanksgiving	thanksgiving
———	may be brought with offering	may be brought with offering

10. Where Do You Stand?

AN EXERCISE COMPARING IDEAS
AND ATTITUDES ABOUT STEWARDSHIP

PURPOSE This activity and planned discussion are intended to raise the awareness of congregational leaders about ideas and attitudes they hold concerning stewardship in the church. The similarities and differences discovered between and among clergy and laity will help develop a definition of stewardship and effective programs and practices of stewardship in the church.

Introduction

For many people in the congregation, stewardship means giving money and the annual financial campaign for pledges. Pastors and laypeople often have different ideas about the purpose and use of money in the church. They often have similar feelings when it comes to hearing and preaching sermons about stewardship. This activity and the discussion that follows are meant to demonstrate the similarities and differences while exploring a definition of stewardship. This session also leads to a discussion about money matters as part of our faith and our habits of giving.

Preparing the Session

Read through the entire session and consider your own responses to the statements in the exercise and the issues that are raised. Where would you stand on each one? Review the discussion questions. Choose and adapt the questions that will be most relevant and helpful for your group.

When leading the Where Do You Stand exercise, people will be moving about and there will be noise and conversation. Each time everyone is in place for each question, take just a moment to note the range of responses and where clusters of people are standing. More in-depth discussion is planned after going through all eleven questions when everyone is seated again. However, depending on the group size or the group dynamics, an option would be to hold the discussion for each question while still standing in place.

Leading the Session

1. Introduce the session with a brief overview using the information given in the sections above.

2. Explain that the session begins with an exercise that depends on their participation. Then ask clergy and laypeople to go to opposite sides of the room. If there is a noticeable, unequal number of one or the other, or if the number of participants is relatively small, both clergy and laypeople may stand along the same side. Once in place, ask them to respond to the statements you will make by moving along an imaginary sliding scale from 1 to 10. Where they stand along the wall will indicate how strongly they agree or disagree with each statement read. Each statement will likely mean moving to a different spot from the one before.

Choose which end represents 1 and which represents 10. Strong agreement is 10, and strong disagreement is 1. Be sure to explain that the scale of agreement or disagreement runs in the same direction for both sides of the room, clergy and laity, if the number of participants allows for using both sides.

Participants will be able to compare their own responses to others and may be swayed by where they think they ought to stand, but the exercise is intended to at least raise the issues and stimulate thinking about personal attitudes and practices of stewardship. In addition to clergy comparing to other clergy and laypeople comparing to other laypeople, participants will be able to make comparisons between laity and clergy, seeing where attitudes and practices may be much the same or quite different.

3. Read the following twelve statements one at a time. Allow time after reading each one for everyone to move to a place on the scale of agreement or disagreement. Also allow time for people to compare where everyone is standing on the particular statement.

- I think it is important to hear and/or give sermons about stewardship.
- I appreciate and enjoy hearing and/or giving sermons about stewardship.
- I don't mind asking someone to make a pledge or a gift to the church.
- I don't mind being asked to make a pledge or a gift to the church.
- I understand our congregation's budget.
- I am comfortable talking about personal financial matters, my own and those of others.
- I think the church is an appropriate place to talk about money.
- I am comfortable talking about matters of personal faith.
- I think most people manage their finances pretty well.
- It's important to teach children and youth about stewardship.
- I don't mind talking about stewardship to children and youth.
- Stewardship is about money.

4. Ask everyone to be seated again for a discussion around each of the issues raised in the exercise. Begin the discussion by asking for general impressions and reactions to the exercise. Note similarities and differences in responses and perceptions between laity and clergy.

Lead into the following subjects for a more in-depth discussion:

Stewardship sermons

How often are stewardship sermons preached in your church? Is there reluctance to preach and/or listen? Who *minds* stewardship sermons more, preachers or the rest of the congregation?

Asking for pledges and gifts

When is it easier to ask or give—when a friend asks or when it is someone you know only slightly? What difference does it make when an explanation of the budget is included and how monies are used?

Understanding budgets

How can budgets be made more understandable for church leaders, governing bodies, and the whole congregation? (For example, line item or narrative)

Money and the church

Is it always appropriate to talk about money in the church? Is it ever appropriate? Can we talk about our personal money issues in the church? With whom? Should money and the church be a private or a public issue?

Personal faith and stewardship

In what ways do issues of gratitude and trust enter into our attitudes and practices of stewardship? Are financial life and spiritual life ever separate?

Talking about stewardship

How are children and youth included in stewardship education and financial campaigns in your congregation? Is it easier to talk to children and youth about money than to other adults? Why might that be? Discuss the importance of serving as role models, whether intentionally or unintentionally, as children and youth observe what we say and do. Discuss the role of the church in dealing with personal or family money matters.

5. Continue the group discussion by developing a definition of the word *stewardship*. Ask for words and phrases that describe stewardship. Compile a list on newsprint or a chalkboard for the group to see.

6. After building the list, read the following definition:

Reflecting upon the word [steward], we might conclude that stewardship has not only to do with money, budgeting, and finances, but with the whole ordering of our life, our corporate deployment of God's varied grace in the daily life of the world. —Douglas John Hall, *The Steward: A Biblical Symbol Come of Age*

Use the following questions for discussion:

- How does this definition compare to the list made by the group?
- What in this definition is particularly different or new for you?
- In what ways is it helpful? Confirming? Challenging?

Closing

Conclude the session with a prayer and/or responses from the group to one or more of the following statements:

- If I had fifteen seconds to tell someone what stewardship means, I would say . . .
- A new understanding I have gained from this exercise and discussion is . . .
- The thing about stewardship that still troubles me is . . .

A Final Word

Stewardship, when fully understood, is living faithfully. It is a perspective on life that sets priorities according to God's ways. It sets the parameters of our choices. Stewardship guides our lives as individuals and as communities, even the world and all creation. And it offers new meaning, new purpose, and joyful fulfillment as we seek to become the persons God created us to be.

Challenges and support for becoming a steward seldom come out of the routine conversations we have or the reading we do. And given that adults are inclined to pursue further education that is useful and immediately important, a conscious effort has to be made to even bring up the subject of stewardship.

The church has potential for being the most appropriate and effective place for challenge, growth, and transformational learning. The church is intentional about its foundation and framework of faith. The community of faith is defined by its search for meaning (according to God's purpose), its openness to question and struggle, and its sharing of stories, beliefs, and hopes. This community not only allows for interaction, reflection and dialogue, but also encourages all of it. The church not only provides for times of learning but also, by its nature and purpose, requires action to follow as both a sign and a commitment to what has been learned that has brought about a change.

Stewardship education can be a vital part of Christian education programs in the church. There are many opportunities for raising the subject of stewardship for study, reflection, and discussion among leaders and other members of congregations, presbyteries, and synods. Although there is value in using a holistic understanding of stewardship, open discussion and study of *financial* stewardship is particularly lacking in our churches when exploring the meaning of personal and corporate discipleship.

Money, wealth, and possessions have always been matters of concern, beyond the needs for safety and survival. Relationships, social standing, political power, a sense of security and, to some extent, hopes for the future are defined or influenced by money. All this can be seen in our contemporary society—its values and the growing disparity among people of different economic levels and among nations.

The Bible has always been a source of guidance for how we are to value money. Its lessons describe the life of faith as the life of a *steward*—a manager or caretaker of the gifts God has given in the created world. Where specific direction for managing money may not be evident in biblical teaching, there is still a description of a world that is to live according to God's economy.

As Christians, we are called to live *as if* we are already a part of God's economy—an economy in which everyone is respected for the work and the gifts he or she contributes, everyone has enough to eat and to stay warm and safe, and everyone enjoys the gifts they have received from God and finds pleasure in sharing them with others. We are to live *as if* our personal, family, church, and community lives are part of, but *only* part of, the household of God, which is the whole creation.

In this household we share responsibility not only for the life we have now, but also for the life we might have or might create together in the future. This life is a series of learning experiences that lead to insight, wisdom, and transformation. When we gather as a Christian community to worship, study, and serve, we join our desires to live more faithfully. We become true stewards of our time, energy, imagination, abilities, opportunities, relationships—and our money, wealth, and possessions in the life of the household of God.

Together, may we discover the true price of faith as we grow in wisdom, offer hospitality to all, and share with one another the blessings, struggles, and joys of living as faithful stewards.